Drawn by E. Jappe, age 86
23 July 1975, Phase Two, time-confused

Available from the Publisher:

Edward Feil Productions, LLC
4614 Prospect Avenue
Cleveland, Ohio 44103

Library of Congress Catalog Number: 2015902801
ISBN #: 978-0-692-37158-9

V/F
VALIDATION®

The Feil Method

How To Help Disoriented Old-Old

by

Naomi Feil, ACSW

Revised with Vicki de Klerk-Rubin

To Ed Feil whose films are
worth a million words.

With grateful acknowledgment to
Piet de Klerk for his insight and
expertise
in the revision of this book

PREFACE

Here's to a wise old age!

This book is for all those who care for and about disoriented old-old people.

Validation helps helpers become comfortable with disoriented old-old who freely express feelings.

Validation accepts people as they are.

Validation helps us understand the reason behind the behavior.

Validation helps the disoriented old-old reach *their* goals-not ours.

BIOGRAPHY

Naomi Feil, M.S.W., A.C.S.W., is the Executive Director of the Validation Training Institute, in Cleveland, Ohio. She is the creator of Validation, currently recognized as a state-of-the-art method of treatment for older people diagnosed as having dementia of the Alzheimer's type or related disorders.

Mrs. Feil earned her master's of social work from Columbia University and studied at the New School for Social Research, Case Western Reserve University, and the University of Michigan. In 1963, she became dissatisfied with traditional therapies for older people with dementia and began to develop her own method for helping older people cope with the disorientation that is sometimes part of the aging process.

In addition to her second book on Validation "The Validation Breakthrough", revised in 2002, Ms. Feil has published numerous journal articles and has produced nine award-winning films on Validation. Mrs. Feil is internationally recognized for her work with older people and is one of the most sought-after trainers in the field. More than 30,000 facilities in the United States, Canada, Europe and Australia work with Validation, and nearly 100,000 professional and family caregivers have attended her workshops in North America, Australia, Europe and Japan. There are 20 Validation centers in 10 countries.

Vicki de Klerk-Rubin is the European manager of the Validation Training Institute, a certified Validation Master and the co-author of The Validation Breakthrough, revision. She has published numerous articles on Validation as well as helped design the Validation course curriculums. Ms. de Klerk-Rubin holds a bachelor of fine arts from Boston University, a master of business administration from Fordham University, and is a Dutch-trained registered nurse. Ms. de Klerk-Rubin gives Validation workshops, lectures and training programs in Europe, the Middle East and the United States.

Notes on this new edition

This revision introduces the newly revised Validation Principles. The new Principles integrate the theories of Erikson and Maslow and focus more on the work of Naomi Feil. These principles now directly relate to a Validation practitioner's behavior and actions, and help us understand the behavior of Maloriented and disoriented very old people. Changes were made to the list of basic human needs. We focused more on what we actually see in daily practice with old people, rather than strictly following Maslow's original hierarchy of needs. The list of research studies on Validation was up-dated to include more recent publications. In addition to these significant changes, small errors were corrected. Should you, the reader, find more errors, please send them to: vdeklerk@vfvalidation.org.

Additional study on the theme of basic human emotions has also led to expanding the list to include more than love, anger, fear and sadness. Currently there is no agreed upon list of 'universal or basic human emotions' among professionals however one could also include disgust, surprise and pain.

Vicki de Klerk-Rubin
The Hague, January 2015

Table of Contents

PART ONE:

WHAT IS VALIDATION?

The Beginning

In 1963, after seven years of working with oriented, healthy elderly in community centers, I began working with old-old people that is, people over the age of 80, who were disoriented, at the Montefiore Home for the Aged in Cleveland, Ohio.[1] My initial goals were to help severely disoriented old-old to face reality and relate to each other in a group. In 1966, I concluded that helping them to face reality is unrealistic. Each person was trapped in a world of their own fantasy.[2] Exploring feelings and reminiscing encouraged group members to respond to each other. Music stimulated group cohesion and feelings of well-being. I abandoned the goal of reality orientation when I found group members withdrew, or became increasingly hostile whenever I tried to orient them to an intolerable present reality.

One very disoriented old-old woman used to sing, "Daisy, Daisy, I'm half crazy..." and then explained the reason for her "dementia", "It's better when you're crazy. Then it doesn't matter what you do."

Another disoriented group member rose to leave the room, saying, "I have to go home now to feed my children." I said, "Mrs. Kessler, you can't go home. Your children are not there. You now live in a home for older people, the Montefiore Home." She answered, "I know that. Don't be stupid! That's why I have to leave this place. Right now. I have to go to my own home to feed my children!" No amount of presentation of present reality could convince Mrs. Kessler. She felt useless in a nursing home. She wanted her own home and her old role as mother of her three children to feel useful. She withdrew from me, muttering to herself, "What does she (pointing to me) know. Who does she think she is!"

[1] Naomi Feil, "Group Therapy in a Home for the Aged," The Gerontologist 7, No.3, Part 1 (September 1967): 192-195.
[2] Edward Feil, The Tuesday Group, film (Cleveland, Ohio: Edward Feil Productions, 1972).

Mr. Rose accused the administrator of the Montefiore Home of castrating him in the attic. I tried to orient Mr. Rose to reality for five years. When the administrator retired, Mr. Rose said to me, "You're right. He didn't hurt me. I'm no good. I never was."

Those were the last words he spoke to me. He dropped his cane and never walked again. On the arm of his wheelchair he walked with his fingers, muttering, "Buckeye and 105th," over and over again. Buckeye and 105th was the corner where his law office had been located. He repeatedly pounded his left knee, which hurt him because of Paget's Disease, saying, "Damn Judge...Damn Judge...Damn Judge..." His father had told him years ago, "You'll never amount to anything. You're no good." His sister told me he never accomplished much. Like a good boy, he bottled up his rage, hurt and guilt. He listened to his father. His father had castrated him with words. The administrator had become a symbol for his father.

Now, in his old-old age, all alone in his wheelchair, he struggled to resolve his rage and guilt. He had entered the final life stage of resolution. I never listened when he blamed his father figures for hurting him. He wanted me to validate his rage. He blamed the judge, the administrator, the doctors, God (his father figures), for ruining his life. His father had punished him in the attic. He returned to the past to tell his father how he felt; to re-store his father's love; to justify himself in this world. Nobody validated him. He struggled alone. His body movements grew feeble. Slowly he lost his purpose for living, and vegetated until death. He moved from phase one, malorientation, to phase four, vegetation, invalidated.[3]

Mr. Rose and hundreds like him taught me to abandon reality orientation with these disoriented old-old. I learned Validation from the people with whom I worked. I learned that they have the wisdom to survive by returning to the past.

---

[3] Naomi Feil, "History of Isadore Rose." Unpublished Case History Montefiore Home, Cleveland, Ohio, 1963-71, available from Author.

Basic Beliefs

To validate is to acknowledge the feelings of a person. To validate someone is to say that his or her feelings are true. Denying feelings invalidates the individual. Validation uses empathy to tune into the inner reality of the disoriented old-old. Empathy, or walking in the shoes of the other, builds trust. Trust brings safety. Safety brings strength. Strength renews feelings of worth. Worth reduces stress. With empathy, the Validation worker picks up clues and helps put feelings into words. This validates the older person and restores dignity.

Some disoriented old-old no longer need to return to the past when they feel strong, loved and worthwhile in present time. Others choose to remain in the past. There is no single or simple formula for everyone. All feel happier when validated.[4]

Validation is a combination of:

- a basic, empathetic attitude
- a late life theory for old-old mal- and disoriented people which helps us understand their behavior
- specific techniques to help mal- and disoriented very old people regain dignity both through individual Validation and through Validation groups

Long Term Validation Goals:

- maintain older people in their own homes
- restore self-worth
- reduce stress
- justify living
- work towards resolving unfinished conflicts from the past
- reduce the need for chemical and physical restraints
- increase verbal and non-verbal communication
- prevent withdrawal inward to vegetation

[4] Naomi Fed, "A New Approach to Group Therapy." Unpublished paper presented at the 25th Annual Meeting of the Gerontological Society in San Juan, Puerto Rico, December, 1972.

- improve gait and physical well-being
- give joy and energy to caregivers
- help families communicate with disoriented relatives.

Validation Principles

Principles: are created by Naomi Feil, apply to maloriented and disoriented elderly; they help guide our actions and determine the Validating Attitude.

V/W Actions/Validation Worker behavior: flow out of the Principles and support the Validation techniques.

Theoretical assumptions/bases: are created by other theorists, apply to the general population (not specific to disoriented elderly) and are useful in supporting Validation Principles when challenged by scientists or academics.

1. All very old people are unique and worthwhile.

Example: *A 90 year old woman lives in a nursing home. The caregiver calls her "sweetie"or mama or grandma."*
Validation: *caregivers address her as "Mrs. Smith."*

V/W action: we address older people in a respectful way and treat each person as an individual.

Theory: from Humanistic psychology (Maslow, Rogers, etc.): know your client as a unique individual.

2. Maloriented and disoriented old people should be accepted as they are: we should not try to change them.

Example: *a 90 year old woman demands her breakfast after she has just eaten. The nurse does not say: "Honey, its 8 o'clock. You just finished all your breakfast. You can't be hungry".*

Validation: *we know that this woman is perhaps psychologically hungry for her family, for love. We ask, 'what fills you up?'*

V/W action: we do not try to change the person's behavior; we accept it and try to help the individual fulfill the needs that are being expressed.

Theory: from Humanistic psychology (Rogers, Maslow, etc.): accept your client without judgment.

Additionally, Freud said that the therapist cannot give insight or change behavior if the client is not ready to change *or does not have the cognitive capacity for insight.*

3. Listening with empathy builds trust, reduces anxiety and restores dignity.

Example: A woman angrily declares that the caregiver threw a basin of water over her clothes and now she's all wet. The trusted, familiar Validation caregiver rephrases, asks, 'Does that happen every morning? 'Yes, every morning.' 'Is there a morning when she doesn't throw water over you?' 'Well, only when the very, nice, young lady comes to look in on me in the night. She asks if I need to go to the toilet. You see, I'm getting older now and I have a problem sometimes with pee-pee.'

V/W action: we understand that this woman is ashamed of being incontinent and empathize with the feelings of the older person without concentrating on the 'truth' of the facts.

Theory: from Humanistic psychology, most especially Rogers who focused his client-centered approach on using empathy.

4. Painful feelings that are expressed, acknowledged and validated by a trusted listener will diminish. Painful feelings that are ignored or suppressed will gain in strength.

Example: An old woman gets up at 3:30 every afternoon to go home to her children. When staff says, 'Sit down. Everything's OK.' She gets more and more nervous and upset. When staff asks, "What is the worst thing that can happen to your children?" The old woman expresses her vivid memory of having left her children alone. Her fears are expressed to a validating caregiver and the old woman feels relieved.

V/W action: we are open to all feelings that are expressed by older people. Through empathy we share these feelings and encourage expression. We acknowledge that disoriented older people freely express emotions in order to heal themselves.

Theory: from Psychoanalytical psychology (Freud, Jung, etc.): "the cat ignored becomes a tiger"

5. There is a reason behind the behavior of very old maloriented and disoriented people.

Example: *A woman accuses the cook of poisoning the food. The nurse does not say, "We have the best cook from Paris." The nurse knows the old woman may have been overfed by her mother (instead of loved), and now she expresses anger against the cook. The validating caregiver asks, "What does she put into the soup?"*

Example: *An old woman refuses to eat soup and vomits each time she is forced to do so. As a Jewish woman during WWII, she hid her identity papers in the soup tureen during a raid at her home.*

V/W action: although we do not always know why the person behaves in a certain way, we help him or her express emotions to resolve unfinished business.

Theory: The brain is not the exclusive regulator of behavior in very old age. Behavior is a combination of physical, social and intrapsychic changes that happen during the life span. (Adrian Verwoerdt is the original source for this, but this idea has been generally accepted by most geriatricians.)

6. The reasons that underlie the behavior of maloriented or disoriented very old people <u>can</u> be one or more of the following basic human needs:

- Resolution of unfinished issues, in order to die in peace
- To live in peace
- Need to restore a sense of equilibrium when eyesight, hearing, mobility and memory fail.
- Need to make sense out of an unbearable reality: to find a place that feels comfortable, where one feels in order or in harmony and where relationships are familiar.

- Need for recognition, status, identity and self-worth
- Need to be useful and productive
- Need to be listened to and respected.
- Need to express feelings and be heard.
- Need to be loved and to belong: need for human contact
- Need to be nurtured, feel safe and secure, rather than immobilized and restrained.
- Need for sensory stimulation: tactile, visual, auditory, olfactory, gustatory, as well as sexual expression
- Need to reduce pain and discomfort

And so they are drawn to the past or are pushed from the present in order to satisfy their needs. They: resolve, retreat, relieve, relive, express.

Example: *A very disoriented woman kisses her hand. The hand is a symbol of her baby. The woman had an abortion, and now needs to express her guilt. She may not be able to see her hand or be aware of her body's position in space. Her hand feels soft, as if it were her baby. She sees her baby with her mind's eye to resolve her guilt and restore her identity as a good mother.*

Example: *An old woman moves her fingers like she used to use her typewriter, to maintain her dignity and identity as a typist. She cannot bear being old without a job. To restore balance, she works. A validating caregiver asks, "You certainly did a lot of typing in your life, didn't you?"*

V/W action: We accept that very old people are in the final life stage, 'Resolution'; we accompany them in the process; we accept that they are often in a personal reality and see this as a wise and healing response to an unbearable present reality.

Theory: several theories back up this principle:
Maslow's hierarchy of needs
Erikson's life task theory
From Humanistic psychology: human beings struggle for balance/homeostasis, and are motivated to heal themselves (Rogers particularly)

7. Early learned behaviors return when verbal ability and recent memory fails:

Example: movement of tongue, teeth and lips create new word combinations–it is often an expression of basic human needs; an old woman sucks on her fingers to feel safe and pleasure (like she felt as a baby) and it is self-stimulating–she is alive.
- *early learned movement can replace speech when verbal ability fails.*

A woman moans: HEALVEN. She tells the worker she needs help from heaven. Her mother is in heaven. She combines images and sounds to form, HEALVEN. The worker asks, "You really miss your mother. Was she always with you when you needed help?"

V/W action: We calibrate the breathing, movements, gestures, body tension, mirror movements and sounds. That allows us to get onto the same wavelength as the old person and meet them where they are in that moment, even if we can't explain their behavior logically.

Theory: Piaget's theory: movement comes before speech in human cognitive development.

8. Personal symbols used by maloriented or disoriented elderly are people or things (in present time) that represent people, things or concepts from the past that are laden with emotion.

Example:
Person: An old man who has been oppressed by his father, accuses the administrator of tying him up at night; a doll is treated like a baby.
Concept: A wedding ring can represent love, a handbag, the identity or self.
Object: An institutional hall can become a street, a wheelchair can become an auto, an old man who used to be a car mechanic gets under his bed every day to repair a car.

V/W action: we accept that symbols are used to express needs and feelings; we try to explore and react with empathy.

Theory: Freud and Jung wrote extensively about symbols, describing them as representations.

9. Maloriented and disoriented old people live on several levels of awareness, often at the same time.

Example: *An old woman runs out of the nursing home calling, 'mama'; she needs to find her mother. When asked, 'Where is your mother?' the old woman says, "My mother is with the dear Lord."*

V/W action: we never lie to older people because we know that on some level they know what is the truth.

Theory: Freud, preconscious, conscious and unconscious

10. When the 5 senses fail, maloriented and disoriented elderly stimulate and use their 'inner senses'. They see with their 'mind's eye' and hear sounds from the past.

Example: *A mother hears her children calling her–she wants to be a good mother to her children. The validating caregiver asks, "How many children do you have?"*

Example: An old mother hears her daughter crying next door. This happens every night. Her 17 year old daughter died and the mother never had enough time to grieve. She wants to express her guilt. The caregiver asks, "What do you miss the most?"

V/W action: when older people see or hear things that we do not, we accept those as being part of their personal reality and understand that they are trying to meet their human needs.

Theory: Wilder Penfield: Human beings can stimulate their brains to recreate vivid visual, auditory and kinesthetic memories.

11. Events, emotions, colors, sounds, smells, tastes and images create emotions, which in turn trigger similar emotions experienced in the past. Old people react in present time, the same way they did in the past.

Example: *A woman hides behind the sofa scared to death each time the meal cart clatters onto the department. She feels the same fear she felt when tanks clattered through the streets of her hometown and bombed her home when she was 4 years old. The worker asks, "Did something terrible happen?"*

V/W action: we accept and acknowledge that experiences from the past can be triggered and explore the feelings without judgment and with empathy.

Theory: Early, well-established emotional memories survive to very old age. Schettler & Boyd. Proust Was a Neuroscientist, by Jonah Lehrer, 2007, published by Houghton Mifflin Co., NY.

Maslow's Pyramid of Human Needs

Principle 6 (see page 17) refers to Maslow's Pyramid of human needs. Abraham Maslow[5] (1908-1970) was a psychologist who developed a theory about human needs. He said that human beings must first fulfil physiological needs (hunger, thirst, etc.), then safety needs (to feel secure and safe), before striving to fulfil psychological and social needs. He created a hierarchy of needs, which not only seems to apply to oriented and healthy people, but also to disoriented elderly to some extent. Maslow's pyramid of needs does not totally apply to very old, disoriented people, but much of it makes sense and gives us more understanding of them.

Maslow's pyramid	**As applied to disoriented elderly:**
Self-actualization: to realize one's full potential	Resolution of unfinished issues, in order to die in peace. To live in peace.
Aesthetic needs: symmetry, order and beauty	Need to restore a sense of equilibrium when eyesight, hearing, mobility and memory fail.
Cognitive needs: to understand and explore	Need to make sense out of an unbearable reality: to find a place that feels comfortable and where relationships are familiar.
Esteem needs: to achieve, gain approval and recognition	Need for recognition, status, identity and self-worth. Need to be useful and productive. Need to be listened to and respected. Need to express feelings and be heard.
Need to belong and be loved: to feel affiliated with others	Need to be loved and to belong. Need for human contact.
Safety needs: feel secure and safe	Need to be nurtured, feel safe and secure, rather than immobilized and restrained
Physiological needs: hunger, thirst, etc.	Need for sensory stimulation: tactile, visual, auditory, olfactory, gustatory, as well as sexual expression. Need to reduce pain and discomfort

[5] Information on Maslow was taken from R Atkinson et at, Introduction to Psychology, Harcourt Brace Jovanovich College Publishers, 1993 (11th ed.)

Most of our actions are motivated by a need of some sort, as are the actions of maloriented and disoriented people. There is a reason for their behavior. Almost all behavior can be attributed to one of the needs described in the above chart.

Example of the need for status, self-worth, usefulness and identity: Josephine Frank, now 88 years old and maloriented, was a librarian for 60 years. She was an avid reader. Reading gave her feelings of self-worth. When she catalogued books, she felt like a useful human being. Miss Frank is losing her eyesight. Without her eyesight, she feels useless. She was never flexible, never able to generate new activities when her social roles wore out. Unable to face her overwhelming panic, she blames the physician for putting drops in her eyes to reduce her vision.

Example of the need to belong and be nurtured: John Marks' mother died in childbirth. At age 92, he longs for the mother he never had. He is now time confused and has returned to early childhood. He attaches himself to a motherly 80-year-old resident whom he sees as his mother. He will not leave her side. He nuzzles her, follows her and cries when she leaves him.

Example of the need for resolution of unfinished issues in order to die in peace: Rebecca Wolff, age 86 had an abortion when she was 14. She is now in repetitive motion. She rolls her towel in the shape of a baby and nurses it, crying and crooning lullabies in her native Russian. Her need to absolve her guilt and to be a mother drives her night and day.

Example of the need for sensory stimulation and the expression of sexual needs: Jacob Mahler, age 94 moves between time confusion and repetitive motion. He was always a good boy, even as an adolescent always obeying his very strict parents quietly. He sublimated his sexual needs with study. Now, he exposes himself and attempts to touch the breasts of residents and nurses. When he speaks he uses sexual language.

We can recognize from our own experience that expressing emotions also can be seen as a basic human need. The expression of raw emotions, unfiltered, basic and universal is an important need expressed by maloriented and disoriented people.

Basic human emotions:
- love/pleasure/joy/sex
- anger/rage/hate/displeasure
- fear/guilt/shame/anxiety
- sadness/misery/grief
- disgust
- surprise
- pain

If you can understand the need behind the behavior, you can have more empathy with the person you are validating. If you put that need into words, the person will feel understood and accepted.

This forms the basis for several Validation techniques that are described later in this book.

Erik Erikson's Theory of Life Stages and Tasks[6]

Erik Erikson, the famous psychologist created a theory of Developmental Life Stages and Life Tasks, that are based upon the interrelationship of our biological, mental and social capacities and drives. These change as we age. Success in accomplishing a task at a certain age depends on how well we have accomplished the earlier task at an earlier age. We are always struggling to accomplish our tasks from birth to death. This resolution process is seen as a human need in very old age. The resolution of unresolved life tasks is one of the major reasons behind bizarre behavior seen in maloriented and disoriented very old people.

Erikson's Life Stages and Life Tasks[7]

Stage	Psycho-social crisis	Behavior seen in disoriented old-old
Infancy	Basic trust vs basic mistrust HOPE	Blamers feel hopeless, helpless, worthless, fearful of everything new or swallows emotions.
Early Childhood	Autonomy vs Shame, Doubt WILL	Good boys and girls, do not say, "no". Fear of taking risks. Express self-doubt, fear of losing control. Hoarding.
Play Age	Initiative vs Guilt PURPOSE	Afraid of new things. Depression, guilt, crying all the time. Martyrs.
School Age	Industry vs Inferiority COMPETENCE	Blamers, "I'm no good", depression
Adolescence	Identity vs Identity Confusion FIDELITY	Sexual acting out. "A man under the bed." I am who you want me to be. Alternative self, use other name.
Young Adulthood	Intimacy vs Isolation LOVE	Withdrawn into self, isolation from others. Dependency

[6] Erik Erikson, Insight and Responsibility, W.W.Norton & Co., New York, 1964.
[7] Erik H. and Joan Erikson, The Life Cycle Completed, extended version, W.W. Norton & Co., New York 1997.

| Adulthood | Generativity vs Stagnation CARE | Clinging to old, outworn, social roles. Telling others what to do and how to do it. "Working all the time", being useful. Denying aging losses. |
| Old Age | Integrity vs Despair, disgust WISDOM | Depression, disgust with the world. Blaming others for failures. "I'm no good." |

The infant, warm and snuggled against mother's breast, is put down abruptly when the phone rings. Now the infant is cold, hungry, frightened and angry. In infancy we must learn to trust that mother will come back. We will survive the cold, hunger pangs, fury, and fear. Mother proves to us again and again that we are loveable. We can live through hard times. She loves us. We can love ourselves, because we are loveable.

But if the infant cannot be sure that mother will return, it never learns to trust and enters childhood loaded with distrust. In kindergarten the child runs, stumbles, falls and accuses the nearest classmate, "You tripped me on purpose!" As an infant he couldn't count on mother's love, never learned that he was loveable. As a child, he does not love himself and cannot trust himself. Now he is the victim, hunting for a destroyer. He denies responsibility for bad things that happen. This child becomes a blamer. Instead of trusting that they can survive, blamers suspect society of doing them in. When this child becomes an old man who falls because his arthritic knees will no longer hold him, he will blame the cleaning woman for deliberately waxing the floor to make him fall. When this old man's eyes blur, he will blame the maintenance man for putting in defective light bulbs.

Fears that were never faced in childhood reappear in disguise in old age. Present-day fears trigger memories of early fears. The little girl who was locked in a dark closet for a terrified moment by an older brother becomes the old woman who shrieks when her eyes fail, or when she is alone in the dark. A physical loss in old age triggers a memory of an earlier feeling of loss Similar feelings attract each other like a magnet. They fly through time.

In **early childhood** we learn control, over our bodily functions as well as our emotional outbursts. This stage is sometimes called "the first adolescence" or "the terrible twos" Two year old vocabulary is focused on 'mine/yours', 'good/bad', 'I do/you do'. As we gain control, we gain self-esteem, "Look! I did the right thing at the right time in the right place."

But if our parents repeat over and over 'Never mess up!'; if we learn that love needs perfection, never soiling, never spilling, we never learn self-esteem; we dare not trust ourselves to do things right. We add another load to our backpack. We carry shame and self-doubt with us into old age. We hang onto things, hoarding what could be lost, what we might need. An old woman does everything her caregiver says, eager to please, asking every few minutes, "Is this right?" An old man waits patiently all day for others to tell him where to sit, what to eat, what to do. Fearful of being unloved and guilty, some old people deposit their feces in wastebaskets, longing for approval from authority.

Play age encompasses the years after early childhood and before we begin school when we explore the world around us through play. We play cowboy, princess, doctor, teacher or fairy, dramatically trying out all possibilities. Play becomes a way of expressing needs, emotions, working out frustrations or trying out new abilities. We learn to ride a bicycle and then try with no hands. We set up tents out of blankets; coloring books are filled in fanciful colors with little attention to 'staying within the lines'. If we never learned self-esteem we dare not try new things. If our play is put down by parents or interrupted we feel guilty. "Stay in the lines." "Don't make a mess." "Can't you play quietly." "I knew you would fall and dirty your pants." In some instances parents are so anxious to give children a head-start that they try to skip the play and instead teach their children to read or work with numbers only giving praise when the child shows them what they want to see. We learn not to fool around, not to make mistakes. We dare not ride our bikes with no hands or climb to the top of the climbing frame. Those inhibitions, that sense of inadequacy is carried forward in our backpacks to old age. In old age when we can't help making mistakes, when controls loosen, we struggle to hang on. Some become hoarders, gathering possessions to ward off further loss. An old man who fears losing his virility, gathers his canes, knives, keys and wallets. Some blame others "There is a leak in my ceiling. Every time it rains, it drips on my bed and nobody will fix it" says the old woman who can't accept her occasional incontinence. An old woman's purse symbolizes her identity as a mother. Fearful of making mistakes, she stuffs it with toilet paper, sugar, salt, and napkins to hold herself together. The more control she loses, the more she hoards.

School Age: once we go to school we find the pleasure of learning new things and develop a work ethic. There are new role models for us in our teachers as well as historical or fictional figures. We enjoy being productive and work at getting good grades.

If teachers and parents never praise us or worse, always criticize or are never satisfied, we feel incompetent. Nothing we do is good enough. Most children in this situation react in one of two ways, either they become excessively competitive or they give up. The competitive person can never do enough and goes through life in a constant state of battle. When this person reaches old age, when competence normally decreases, he can't handle the loss and will fall back on old coping mechanisms to explain away the failures. This old man barks out orders to nursing home personnel just like he did when he was the boss of a big company. The person who gives up goes through life in a state of inertia, not trying to live up to anyone's expectations because she knows she can never do enough or be good enough. This person has given up before she has even started. This woman lies in bed, refuses to attend activities, fearful of being rejected because she can no longer walk as well as she did; or because she has trouble hearing. Gradually she loses mobility and withdraws inward.

In Adolescence, teenagers must cut the cord, and rebel. When you are 15, mother can turn into a wicked witch and father a dreadful dragon breathing the fire of hated authority. We reject their rules, defy them. We must discover our own values, make up our own rules. We fight to find out who we are; to separate from our loved ones. We've learned in infancy, that our parents love us even when we fight them. We can risk rebellion.

But, if we do not have and hold unconditional love from our parents, rebellion is risky. If we fight and disobey, mother and father might not love us anymore. They might abandon us. We will be alone. Therefore, we capitulate, are good, always do what mommy and daddy want. We never learn who we are-ourselves, separate from our parents, separate from authority. We are the teacher's good student, the boss' good worker. We borrow our identity from the outside world, never having found our own. We never cut the cord. We never learn to "be," without our family, without home, without our legs, in our wheelchairs, all alone. We always have to be somebody's something. This type of old woman clings to her children, to her neighbors, to the nursing home staff. She becomes the martyr; complains about her aches and pains, giving the world her "organ recital," "My head hurts, my stomach hurts, my back aches," and so on. She whines, "One mother can raise ten children, but ten children can't take care of one mother."

In **young adulthood** our task is to get close to another human being. If as a teenager we gained a sense of identity, we can afford to say, "I love you," or, "I hate you," without fear of rejection. Our ability to love is not dependent on being loved. If we are rejected, we will survive. We have our own identity, separate from the loved one. We can risk being hurt. But, if we fail to accomplish our earlier life tasks, we will not reach out for intimacy. If we could never trust ourselves to take our hands off the handlebars as children, how can we trust ourselves to survive the inner bumps of adulthood? Haunted by the terror of abandonment in infancy; the agonizing embarrassment of failure as a child; the fear of rejection as a teenager; we stay apart from others. We become isolated and acquire a new load to carry into old age. We become a recluse. In the nursing home we sit alone. Without stimulation from the outside world, with failing eyesight and hearing, we retreat inward more and more.

In **adulthood** we go through two variations of the same process of generativity. First we generate an 'adult life.' We marry, have children and build a career. As we age and life situations change, we learn to generate new ways of being. Our task in middle age is to roll with the punches. We watch our wrinkles deepen, our hair thin. Our wrinkly skin doesn't fit the bones; the bags under our eyes won't unpack. We look in the mirror. Everything seems the same as it did five years ago, but it's all a little lower. Some of us suffer an onslaught, an avalanche of losses. We lose a spouse, a breast, a kidney, a job...and on and on. We face our losses. We grieve. We look in the mirror and accept the fact that we are aging and will not live forever. In middle age we move on; expand our repertoire for living; add new keys to the piano of our lives. A wife dies; a close friend is found. A job goes; we become a volunteer.

But, if we have learned that we must be perfect, that we cannot lose control, then we cannot spill our gut feelings, our grief to anyone. So, how can we face the wounds of middle age? Without our spouse, we are nobody. Without our job, we are nothing without our breasts, we are sexless. To survive, we deny the impact of our losses. We cannot risk learning new keys, so continue banging the same old key. We hang onto outworn roles. A widower rejects a new relationship'—nobody is good enough. A music lover refuses to buy a hearing aid-it's too expensive. An executive ridicules a volunteer job-his time is worth money. We are stuck clinging to outworn behaviors. In the second phase of resolution (time confusion) a wheelchair becomes a filing cabinet so the executive can continue working; a hand becomes a baby for the woman who must remain a mother. A medicine cart is a tractor for the farmer who needs to plow his field. These very old people must hold onto their jobs. They have nothing else to do. They are locked in because they have only one key.

Erikson says that the life task in **old age** is to review life. It's time to look backward, to sort out what we were. We review the past in order to preview the future. One woman says, "What was I? I was a mother and I made a lot of mistakes, but I learned from my mistakes. I did a lot of good things too." We figure out where we are. Another chimes in, "I am now an old woman. My husband is gone. But, I can share feelings with close friends." We think about what we could have been. A third declares, "I wish I had been a great actress, but I wasn't. Instead, I used my acting skills to become a good teacher. I like myself. Despite my unfulfilled dreams, my mistakes, despite my losses, I am glad I was born. I respect myself. I have integrity. I can compromise. I can accept what I am, what I was and what I wasn't. I like me. Life is worth living. Although I'm in a wheelchair, I am pulling my act together." Those old-old have faced their tasks along the way, and now they deliberately reminisce, accepting the choices they have made, accepting themselves as they are.

Integrity in old age is recognizing one's strengths in spite of weakness. "Integrity is the merger between the actual self and the idealized self" according to Erikson.[8] With integrity, the old person counts on deep self-respect to heal the inevitable bruises that come with age. With integrity, I can risk a new life style when old patterns no longer work.

But, if you can't trust anyone to love you when you begin to lose your physical energy; when your eyes blur, your hair thins, your recent memory wavers, you are retired...then life is a mud puddle and you're stuck in it. You may think, "Nobody cares if I live or die. I wish I were dead." Without deep self-acceptance to outweigh failure, there is despair.

Despair, if ignored, rumbles and turns into depression. Depression is an internal temper tantrum. Rage, rebellion, shame, guilt, love...emotions that have been successfully bottled up for a lifetime, gain strength while locked inside. Bearing a backpack that becomes unbearable, we move towards old-old age. Humans are living longer and longer. The old-old have become a new breed of people. Pneumonia is no longer "the old person's cure at age 65." Statistics show that most of us will reach very old age.

[8] Erik Erikson, Childhood and Society, WW.Norton & Co., New York, 1950, 1963

In his 80's, Erikson came to the conclusion that he had to add a further life stage to his theory. Joan Erikson draws on the work of Lars Tornstam in her revision of her husband's last book, *The Life Cycle Completed.*[9] Gerotranscendence flows from Integrity and is described as a state of withdrawal from usual daily activities, a release from rushing about and the tensions of everyday life. The individual becomes deeply involved in more spiritual matters, not necessarily in a religious sense. Erikson describes a feeling of cosmic communion, an expanded sense of time despite the contracting of physical capability; one accepts death as the natural end to the life cycle and the sense of self expands beyond the ego to encompass mankind.

This remarkable state can only be achieved by people who have the emotional and physical resources to choose their withdrawal instead of feeling isolated by physical deterioration, society's rejection of old-old people and the loss of loved ones. When a person can't handle all the physical, social and psychological losses, withdrawal becomes not a choice, but a defense mechanism.

Each stage of life has its own unique task. Ignore it, and the task makes a second entrance in a later stage. We get second and third chances to accomplish our life tasks. We seldom accomplish a life task the first time around. And no life task is completely finished. You should keep facing your feelings, being honest with yourself throughout life.[10] If, at 62, you fail to find a street in a strange town, and begin to blame the faulty street signs, you can face the fact that you are a blamer. You can express fear of becoming blind to a close friend. You can search for alternative ways of seeing. If you shy away from friendships, face your fear of intimacy, the pangs of rejection. You can change and not stay stuck in old patterns of behavior. Human beings with, millions of brain cells, can regroup and add new connections. Our brains are "plastic." Heat plastic and it changes its shape.

We are struggling throughout life.[11] Seldom is any life task completely accomplished before the next one appears on the

[9] See note 7
[10] Erik H. and Joan M. Erikson, Introduction: Reflections On Aging, in: Stuart Spicker, Kathleen Woodward, David Van Tassel (eds), Aging And The Elderly, Humanities Press, Atlantic Highlands, NJ., 1978
[11] Gail Sheehy, Passages, E.P.Dutton & Co., New York, 1974

scene. We always need to go back to pick up the stray pieces. The unfinished task nags and follows us to very old age. If we continue to deny its existence, if we refuse to face it, the task waits until our controls weaken. We forget our entrance cues. We forget our lines. We have waited too long, it is too late. We lose the desire and the ability to change. Insight, the intellectual grasp of feelings, the "AHA!" is hard enough to achieve when we are physically intact. Facing feelings makes us vulnerable. Facing feelings is scary. We lose balance. In old age, each day brings another physical loss. At 83, we will not risk a heart attack by facing bottled-up feelings that terrify us. If we have ignored our important feelings, they finally flaunt us in our old age, when we have lost our controls and we are at the mercy of our care-givers. Buried for a lifetime, feelings finally erupt.

Feil's Resolution versus Vegetation Stage:
The Stage Beyond Integrity

Old-old Age-Feil	Resolution vs Vegetation DIE IN PEACE	Malorientation Time Confusion Repetitive Motion Vegetation

In 1963, when I returned to work in the nursing home where I grew up, I found that most of the 170 residents were oriented, integrated human beings who had learned to compromise. They rolled with the punches of old age and still enjoyed living, despite physical and intellectual deficiencies. Only 23 residents had become confused or disoriented. Their ages ranged from 80 to 101 years. Nobody wanted them. They were the blamers, the martyrs, moaners, wanderers, yellers, pacers and the pounders. I didn't know it then, but each one had accumulated, during more than seven decades, a backpack of festering feelings. These were the very old people with whom I worked in the Special Service Wing, separated from the oriented residents who resented their "crazy" behaviors. Staff, too, wanted little to do with those very old people who could not or would not control their feelings and conform to society's expectations. In the 1930s, those 23 people would have died of pneumonia or heart disease, but modern medicine kept them alive. They had outlived their bodies.

These very old people gradually taught me that there is yet another task to accomplish in old-old age. I call this final task, the one beyond integrity, Resolution versus Vegetation. Very old people who are stuck with deep unresolved feelings left over from earlier life stages, often return to the past to resolve those feelings. They pack for their final move. They sort out dirty linen stashed in the storehouse of the past. They are busy, irresistibly drawn to wrap up loose ends. This is not a conscious move to the past, like Erikson's old-age stage. It is a deep human need: to die in peace. Those who achieve integrity in very old age never enter the Resolution stage. But, as humans continue to live longer, there will be a growing number of very old people who fall into the final Resolution stage. They need someone to listen, to validate their feelings. If no one listens, they withdraw to Vegetation. With no stimulation from the outside world, they become one of the living dead in our nursing homes. The Validation worker listens, knowing that there will never be a complete resolution; it is too late for insight. Feelings spill, unresolved until death. However, as the various feelings are acknowledged and validated, they dissipate. The old-old continue resolving, always preparing to die in a clean house.

The Reasons for Disorientation:
Denial of Physical and Social Losses

Physical Losses[12]

Physical aging means a gradual loss of useful tissue throughout the body. Human life span ranges to 120 years. People who hold onto outworn youthful roles deny normal signs of aging. Denial begins in middle age when wrinkles appear, skin fits loosely over shrinking bones, hair thins, night driving becomes difficult and some may develop breast tumors, prostate problems, cataracts, have small strokes and heart trouble. Fatty tissue accumulates. Brain and heart work harder. People who have no repertoire for facing losses are stuck. Aging will not stop. Denial of these physical, small "deaths" in middle and old age often leads to a final retreat into fantasy in old-old age.[13] In fact, physical deterioration helps the very old person who has unfinished life tasks, to accomplish the final task: restore the past in order to resolve it.

Loss of hearing causes some people to listen with their inner ear. The little boy, who was constantly ridiculed in kindergarten because he could not control his urine, becomes the deaf old man who hears with his mind's ear. Instead of hearing his friend's playful, "You wanna bet?" the old man hears, "You're wet." The embarrassment of losing his hearing as an adult is like a magnet. It attracts the same feeling of shame he had as a boy when he wet his pants and the children taunted: "Sammy is wet! Sammy is wet!" The old Sam shakes his fist and walks away. He has lost his only friend. Loss of hearing awakens insecurities from the past. The only self-defense is denial for those who cannot face failures. Unsure, they begin to suspect others of ridiculing them. They retreat inward more and more. The former friend calls Sam "paranoid." It becomes easy to hear sounds from the past when the outside world is muffled. To ease his suffering, the old man hears his mother's voice.

[12] Sue V. Saxon, Mary Jean Etten, Physical Change and Aging, Tiresias Press, New York, 1978

[13] James J. Bartell, Donald D. Price, Two Experimental Orientations Toward a Stressful Situation and Their Somatic and Visceral Responses, Psychophysiology 14 (1977): 517-521

If, as an adult, he had worked through that feeling of shame about wetting his pants, he might have accepted his hearing loss as an old man and would not have withdrawn. He would not have the need to resolve unfinished feelings as an old man. Had he struggled with that life task at an earlier stage, he would not have to enter the Resolution stage of life.

Eyes change. When the outside world blurs, the inside world can clear up. In old age, the optic nerve suffers damage, the lens yellows. An old person with a damaged retina can use the mind's eye to see. Vivid (eidetic) images restore loved ones from the past. Schettler and Boyd wrote: "The earlier an image has been imprinted on memory, the longer it is retained."[14] Wilder Penfield found: "The patient, himself, can activate the memory from within..., without the use of the sense organs."[15] Streaks, created by the sun's reflections, become a fence for an 88 year woman whose Daddy warned her to keep the horses inside the fence. Strapped in her chair, seeing with her vivid inner sight, hearing her father's voice with her mind's ear, smelling the past, she shouts: "Daddy, the horses won't listen. They got out! I didn't mean it. Dad! Help!" This old woman resurrects her father to make peace. She is resolving old feelings of guilt. Her family could not afford to lose those horses. In a poetic and creative way she changes present to past time in her final life struggle to regain her father's approval.

The brain changes as we age. There is less glucose and oxygen for brain metabolism. The nervous system is damaged. The old-old person begins to lose control over muscles and glands. Bowel and bladder functions become difficult. The human brain has billions of nerve cells. In our 20s we lose a few thousand. By age 90, some people have suffered considerable damage to the brain. We all age differently, depending upon genetics and environment. Little strokes and damaged nerve cells (plaques and tangles in the brain) can cause recent memory loss. Some very old people lose the ability to think intellectually—to put similar things into

[14] EG. Schettler, G.S. Boyd, Atherosclerosis, North-Holland Publishing CoiBiomedical Press, Amsterdam, 1969

[15] Wilder Penfield, The Cerebral Cortex and the Mind of Man, in: Peter laslett (ed.), The Physical Basis of Mind, Macmillan Co., New York, 1950

categories. When our brains are complete we can easily put chairs, tables and desks into the category of "furniture." We can pass this intelligence test: "A chair is to a table as an apple is to..." Very old people with damaged logical thinking cannot supply a word like "orange" or "banana." They can no longer think cognitively. They can no longer put minutes, hours, days, weeks, months, years, into chronological order. Very old people are governed by memories. They keep track of their lifetime instead of minutes. Present and past blend. Clock time has gone. An old woman who cannot give up her only reason for living, motherhood, shouts, "I want to feed my children. They are hungry." She is told, "You just ate your breakfast. Your children are grown up." She yells louder, has forgotten that she just ate, doesn't want to eat in this sterile institution. This old woman doesn't remember that her children are grown up. She wants to feed them "rocky eggs and fish sticks."

Our sensory system can suffer damage. Sensory cells located throughout the body no longer inform the brain of the body's position. There is a blurring of the sense of self.[16] Dr. Smith no longer recognizes himself in the mirror when he is being shaved. He moves "beside himself." His brain no longer informs him of where he is or who he is. Dr. Smith had controlled his sexual instincts throughout his life. Now, they are finding the light of day. With a wicked gleam and a snicker of glee, he pats the breasts of the nursing assistant who is shaving him. When I asked, "Dr. Smith, do you know that you are making Sally feel uncomfortable?" he shooed me away, saying, "I am not Dr. Smith. Dr. Smith is in his office, practicing medicine. Now leave me alone. I'm busy." With damaged kinesthetic awareness, he uses his mind's eye to see Dr. Smith safely working in his laboratory or practicing medicine, the way he did for decades. Meanwhile, the man who is being shaved is busy working on completing his unresolved sexual feelings before death.

When the brain no longer knows where the body is in present reality, movements can take very old people back to work. If it is

---

[16] N. Feil, J. Flynn, Meaning Behind Movements of the Disoriented Old-Old, Somatics IV, No.2 (Spring/Summer 1983)

imprinted early on and reinforced through the years, our muscle memory stays. A slight flick of the wrist can take an old man back to his job as a carpenter. Motions can trigger emotions. Mrs. Kulp, almost blind, holds her hand to her lips, caressing it, crooning and rocking her "hand baby." Here movements trigger visualizations. Her hand, soft like her baby, becomes her baby, and restores her identity as a mother.

Mr. Rose, a former lawyer, pounds his left knee that hurts him due to Paget's disease. He shouts, "Damn judge, damn judge," eyes focused on his painful knee. His fingers travel up and down the arm of his wheelchair. They are his "feet", marching up and down, never stopping their motion, traveling back to the street where he practiced law. His knee hurts the way the judge hurt Mr. Rose when he lost his one big law case. Now, at 86, Mr. Rose punishes the judge and reviews his case, using familiar motions to restore the past. He is cleaning house before he dies. Patting, crooning, rocking, folding, tongue flicking, stroking, pounding, are physical movements that have a unique meaning to disoriented very old persons. They use familiar body movements to relive the past.

Social Losses

Death of loved ones, loss of one's job, loss of one's role as a worker, a mother, a child, or a friend, deprive old-old people of social stimulation. Touching, eye contact, recognition, and validation from loved ones are basic human needs.[17] With little or no stimulation from the outside world people vegetate or die. Loss of stimulation leads to loss of identity. From infancy to old-old age, we need to interact with others. Stuck in their wheelchairs, some old-old lose touch with the outside world. Without feedback from other people, the old person can no longer match inner perceptions with what is actually happening outside.

Some very old people have always denied social losses. When a loved one died, they repressed the pain. Awareness of that pain would have created intolerable anxiety, caused panic, a flushed face,

[17] Willard Mittelman, Self-Actualization, Journal of Humanistic Psychology 31 (Winter 1991): 114-135

clammy hands, crying, sweating, inability to move, and increased their heartbeat. Pain can cause too much turmoil for very old people to bear. They move inside themselves to survive the stress of facing unbearable reality all alone.

The Wisdom in Disorientation

The outside world blurs. What happens outside no longer matters. There is no one out there who cares. No one to love. Nothing to do. Physical deterioration of vision, hearing, reflective self-awareness and mobility contribute to the inward march. The old-old person no longer expends the energy to remember names of people in the present. Recent memory fades.

Alone in an apartment or trapped in a geriatric chair, they return to the time when they were somebody. They use their vivid memories to restore the past, when they were useful, productive, loved. They go back to a time when what they thought and did really counted. They relive the past to restore their dignity. They no longer care about pleasing people now. They get no satisfaction from present day reality. Human beings need stimulation in order to survive. The old-old stimulate themselves through memory. The past replaces the present. Night-time and daytime blend and overlap with no place to go, nothing to do, and no one to see at any time.

The early way of perceiving the world returns. The old-old go back to the past searching for identity, meaning, to tie up living. They express basic human needs:

- Resolution of unfinished issues, in order to die in peace.
- To live in peace.
- Need to restore a sense of equilibrium when eyesight, hearing, mobility and memory fail.
- Need to make sense out of an unbearable reality: to find a place that feels comfortable and where relationships are familiar.
- Need for recognition, status, identity and self-worth.

- Need to be useful and productive.
- Need to be listened to and respected.
- Need to express feelings and be heard.
- Need to be loved and to belong: need for human contact.
- Need to be nurtured, feel safe and secure, rather than immobilized and restrained.
- Need for sensory stimulation: tactile, visual, auditory, olfactory, gustatory, as well as sexual expression.
- Need to reduce pain and discomfort

But, they no longer express these needs to people in the "here and now." Their communication is with people and objects from their past. They become egocentric, shutting out external reality. Speech centers deteriorate from disuse and from organic damage. They can no longer retrieve dictionary words; no longer define people or objects or relationships. They can no longer put "mother" into a category of "someone who has children." They return to well-established memories of their own mother. Brain circuits dormant since youth, wake up and return to full consciousness. The old woman rocks to bring back her mother. The motion brings emotion. She feels loved. Damage to rational thinking "frees and allows for greater non-verbal expression."[18] [19] When logical, learned speech goes, they return to "primal linguistic patterns."[20] This is not a second childhood. Well-learned memories persist throughout a lifetime. Wilder Penfield found that a stimulation in the present can play back an early memory with complete clarity. We can relive significant sights, sounds, smells and emotions that have been stored in our brain circuits since birth.[21] When speech goes, very old disoriented people communicate with movements learned early in life. Their movements replace speech.

[18] A. Zaidel, The Concept of Cerebral Dominance in the Split Brain, in: E.W. Busse (e&), Cerebral Correlates of Conscious Experience, Elsivier, Amsterdam, 1978: 263-284.

[19] P Wat2Jawick J. Bevin and D.D. Jackson, Pragmatics of Human Communication, W.W. Norton & Co., New York 1967.

[20] See Penfield Note 15.

[21] Russell Brain, Speech and Thought, and Wilder Penfield, The Cerebral Cortex and the Mind of Man, in: Peter Laslett, op. cit.

The Swiss psychologist Piaget found that movements precede speech.[22] When an infant wants his absent mother, he learns to mimic her movements to bring her to mind. She rocked him. In imitating mother's rocking motion, he feels her presence. The rocking motion becomes the mother. At six months, the infant learned to imitate the sucking movements involved in nursing to remind himself of his mother. By moving his tongue and lips together, he has found his mother and is comforted. In school, when the structures in the brain are completely formed, the child learns to define the word "mother." He begins to understand how to classify. A mother belongs in a category of anyone who has offspring. A puppy can have a mother, too. The word "mother" is classified and stored in the left brain. The child learns to think in the abstract, using dictionary words instead of made-up words to replace the actual objects. The sucking movement is stored in his permanent memory and forgotten intellectually. The child becomes a social animal.

In very old age, the disoriented person having lost those dictionary words returns once more to well established, permanently stored movements. They move their lips to combine similar sounds and begin to rhyme as the sounds blend with one another. Like a finger painter, they smear vowels and consonants together that feel good, harmonize and are pleasurable to the tongue, teeth and lips. Childhood phrases, poems, prayers and songs return to very old people who cannot speak.

Further deterioration to intellectual functions also brings an increase in unique personal words which are a passage to the past. Early memories return to vivid consciousness. Mrs. Gogolick, peering at a curtain in the nursing home, says: "That's symofile contabulation in the Fendall Company!" I discovered the meaning behind her unique word formations after ten years and much consultation with a linguist. My name is "Feil". Mrs. Gogolick was a file clerk. The curtain in my "Feil" company in the present was similar to the curtain in her "file clerk" office of the past. She smeared these sounds together to create her unique word: "symofile." Mrs. Gogolick had been a bookkeeper, added up

[22] Jean Piaget, The Origins of Intelligence in Children, W.W. Norton & Co., New York, 1952

figures, tabulated. She "figured out" or "tabulated" her observation about the curtain and created a new word, "contabulation." Her word doodle, "Fendall," is a combination of the phrase: "Memorable friends from the past." Mrs. Gogolick communicates by using her personal vocabulary.

Disoriented very old people move through the past resolving unfinished relationships. They express their uncontrollable feelings through movements and unique word formations.

Disorientation is regression, but the old person is not a child. The child can change and grow, wants to learn new facts, new words, can play games using established adult rules. The child is capable of cognitive reasoning, can learn to classify people and objects, and wants to compare things that are alike and things that are different. The child learns to tell clock time, becomes aware of schooltime, playtime, and bedtime. It also learns to be self-aware and aware of others, can learn to control feelings and listen to the adult. Care-givers must teach children, give them roots, help them grow.

Disoriented old-old people have already rooted and grown. With the wisdom of crystallized human experience and intuition, they return to the past to clean house and to meet their basic human needs for love and identity. No longer willing to conform to society's rules, they review their earlier experiences according to their own rules. Returning to the past enables them to avoid the painful present, their feelings of uselessness and aloneness. They will not be aware of the present: day, time or place. Why keep track of chronological time when there is no place in it for you? They will not respond to efforts of young nursing home workers who try to change behaviors according to the standards of a young, productive society. The old-old return to their roots and ignore or get angry at people who will not listen to them or argue with them. They prevent vegetation by restoring the past. That is how the disoriented old-old survive.

Who are the Disoriented Old-Old?

Disoriented old-old are very old people who:

- have inflexible behavior patterns
- hold onto outworn roles
- have to grapple with unfinished feelings
- withdraw from present day reality to survive
- have significant cognitive deterioration and can no longer function intellectually to achieve insight

This population benefits from Validation.

The disoriented old-old are people who have led more or less useful, productive, satisfying lives and have no history of severe mental illness. They functioned well before being overpowered by so many losses. Ravaged by the loss of sight, hearing, recent memory, social roles, jobs, homes, and mobility, they withdraw, rather than acknowledge so many losses. Overcoming adversity through denial has worked before to help them survive life's crises. In very old age, when one crisis follows another, overloading and ganging up on them, such people retreat from reality. They have no other way of coping. Like a person lost in a storm, the disoriented very old retreat into the past to find safe shelter. The past eases present-day pain, brings back nostalgia, familiar streets, loved ones, work. There are few rewards in living in a wheelchair in a nursing home. Mrs. Kessler turns her back on young workers who want to orient her to present-day reality. She explains her return to the past in the film, *Looking for Yesterday*[23]: "I'm looking for yesterday to untangle the noodles in the mirrors of my mind." This old-old woman was diagnosed "demented." Dementia comes from the Latin "dis," meaning away from, and "mens," the mind. Hence: "out of the mind," or "mind-less." Without a mind, Mrs. Kessler, an 86-year-old Russian peasant woman, could not have been that poetic. Having lost most of her speech and logic, she moved in realms of personal feelings, freely associating words, sounds, and body movements to express herself.

[23] Edward Feil, Looking for Yesterday, film (Cleveland, Ohio: Edward Feil Productions, 1978)

Bottled-up emotions spilled. The cork popped. Validation means acknowledging and respecting the behavior of very old disoriented people, who express themselves poetically, rather than logically.

Validation helps people who have the following characteristics, no matter what medical diagnosis is given. These are the disoriented old-old:

- 80+ years of age[24]
- have no history of psychiatric problems
- the disorientation is not caused by a physical illness i.e. Parkinson's, Korsakov, early onset Alzheimer, Pick's, urinary infection, drug intolerance, dehydration, vitamin deficiency, etc.

Disorientation stems from a combination of losses and the inability to cope with the losses:

Physical losses:

- Damage to brain, senses (vision, hearing, feeling (tactile), smelling, tasting).
- Often have diminished ability to move.

Psychological losses:

- Denied severe losses throughout their lives.
- Unresolved life tasks or crises demand attention.
- Short-term memory is replaced by long-term memory.

Social losses:

- Status is diminished by society.
- Important roles are lost (mother, teacher, home-owner, etc.).

---

[24] Age is relative and we all grow old differently. One 90-year old looks and acts as if she were 70. A 60-year old behaves as if he were 90, therefore, 80+ is a generalization. There are many exceptions to the rule. I have discovered through my practice that most people over 80 begin to suffer some degree of physical deterioration that is related to aging. They also begin to wrap up their experiences in order to die in peace.

Each person is unique and responds differently to physical and social changes that happen to everyone in old-old age. People differ more from each other in old age than in any other life stage. Categorizing disoriented old-old in one package, labeled "dementia" or the currently popular label "Alzheimer's type dementia" often leads to the use of inappropriate methods of helping them. Methods that do not work. Some very old people can roll with the punches and remain oriented despite severe damage to brain structure. Others, with similar brain damage become very disoriented.[25] The condition of the brain, is only one criterion, and does not provide enough information to make an accurate diagnosis.[26] A person's behavior in old age is influenced by his/her acquired repertoire of coping methods plus a combination of physical and social losses.

Individuals with a wide variety of behavior patterns have the best chance for success when faced with physical deterioration in old-old age.[27] These very old people do not need Validation: they validate themselves throughout life.

Validation was not developed for people who:

- are oriented
- are mentally handicapped
- have a history of mental illness
- have suffered an organic trauma (i.e.: aphasia after a stroke or fall)
- are not old-old

These people are either capable of changing their acting-out behavior or the behavior does not come from an inability to deal with an overwhelming number of losses. The goal of the helper is to facilitate change through confrontation, behavior modification, or insight. The goal of Validation is not to give insight or to confront because disoriented old-old people are no longer capable of cognitive thinking. However, Validation principles: empathy, warmth, respect, know your client and understand their goals,

---

[25] J.B. Aker, Arthur C. Walsh and J.R Beam, Mental Capacity, Medical and Legal Aspects of Aging, McGraw-Hill Book Co., New York, 1977

[26] Adrian Veiwoerdt, Clinical Geropsychiatry, Williams & Wilkins Co., Baltimore, Md., 1976

[27] Julius Weil, Special Program for the Senile in Home for the Aged, Geriatrics 21 (January 1966): 197-202

apply to most helping methods and Validation techniques can help.

Diagnostic Labeling

Dementia

Dementia is a term that was first used in the early nineteenth century by the French researchers Pinel (1745-1826) and Esquirol (1772-1840) to describe mental deterioration and idiocy caused by lesions in the brain. "Senile dementia" was seen as the progressive deterioration of the brain in aging. These days the word 'dementia' is used in professional literature"[28] as an umbrella term for a combination of symptoms. It describes a chronic and progressive deterioration in higher cortical or cognitive abilities. This includes memory, thinking, orientation, comprehension, calculation, learning ability, use of language and judgment. Often loss of emotional controls, social behaviors and personality changes accompany the cognitive losses. Dementia can be caused by a number of diseases or medical conditions such as: vascular or multi-infarct (caused by many strokes), HIV/AIDS, drug abuse, head trauma, Parkinson's disease, Huntington's disease, Alzheimer's disease, Pick's disease and Korsakov's syndrome (alcohol induced dementia). There are also many cases of dementia where no disease or medical condition can be identified through testing.

There is much confusion in the terminology. Over the last 30 years, different terms have been used to describe older people who have symptoms of dementia. 'Senile dementia', 'presenile dementia,' 'chronic organic brain syndrome,' and Alzheimer-type dementia' are most often listed under 'medical diagnosis' in patient charts. In fact the names used to describe patients with the same symptoms, change according to region and country. One of the reasons for this confusion is that this field is quite dynamic and

---

[28] DSM V, American Psychiatric Association Diagnostic & Statistical Manual of Mental Disorders, 2013, as well as P Wright, J. Stern, M. Phelan (ed), Core Psychiatry, W.E. Saunders Company London, 2000

new discoveries are being made every year. New information leads to new nomenclature. There are two widely used manuals for diagnostic classification: the *Diagnostic and Statistical Manual of Mental Disorders* (DSM,) which is published by the American Psychiatric Association, and the *ICD Classification of Mental and Behavioral Disorders* (ICD), published by the World Health Organization. These two books offer very specific diagnoses and describe how one might identify each disease or condition. These guidelines are periodically updated according to the latest research and are often used as the basis for insurance reimbursement. In other words, if the illness is listed in the *DSM* or *ICD,* costs will be reimbursed. It has been known to occur that patients are diagnosed with Alzheimer's disease for insurance purposes. Other sad facts are that diagnostic guidelines are not always followed and there is often no money to do the necessary testing that would allow professionals to make a diagnosis.

Disoriented very old people are often mis-diagnosed because of a lack of proper testing and a failure to use the most up-to-date, accepted guidelines. Even with proper testing, it is difficult to make an accurate diagnosis because people often have more than one condition. The damage caused by one illness could mask the symptoms of another illness.

Alzheimer's disease

In 1906, Alois Alzheimer, analyzing the brain of a 51 year old woman, observed that there were "remarkable changes in the neurofibrils ... and a peculiar substance in the cerebral cortex," and concluded that he was confronted with a distinctive disease process. This process was called "Alzheimer's Disease" by Alzheimer's mentor, Kraepelin. Deterioration as a result of this disease is rapid, and the earlier the onset, the more severe its course.[29] Butler and Lewis describe the decline as follows: "First, loss of cognition, then, aphasia, emotional liability, a Parkinsonism-like gait and convulsive seizures, with increasing difficulty in swallowing.

[29] Marian Emr, Progress Report on Senile Dementia of the Alzheimer's Type, NI11 Publication No. 81-2342, National Institute on Aging, Rockville, Md., September 1981

Eventually utter helplessness prevails, with incontinence and marasmus. Onset takes place in the forties or fifties and an individual seldom lives longer than four or five years after the illness begins?"[30] Therefore, people with Alzheimer's disease seldom reached the age of 65. They died, mainly of pneumonia or heart disease, because their immune systems were affected.

In the pre-1978 categorization, Alzheimer's disease was one of the common forms of presenile dementia. The diagnosis was ultimately based on autopsy. If neurofibrillary plaques and tangles were found in the brain, a person was diagnosed as "Alzheimer's." Neurofibrillary tangles, first described by Alzheimer in Munich in 1906, are abnormally paired fibers, twisted filaments, on a neuron. Senile plaques, first found in 1898 by Redlich on degenerating neuron cell processes, are deposits of an amyloid protein which accumulate around brain cells and cause damage.

More recently other markers of early onset Alzheimer's disease have been discovered. There are neurochemical changes, a reduction of choline acetyltransferase and other neurotransmitters or neuromodulators. Genetic markers have been identified that indicate an increased risk of developing the disease. These are not definitive signs of the disease, but support information found on autopsy. According to press releases in January 2002,[31] UCLA scientists have discovered what they call a 'tracer molecule' called FDDNP which attaches itself to plaques in the brain. When one then uses positron emission tomography (PET scan) the brain damage can be seen in living people. Should this diagnostic tool be proven to be accurate, it would be the first time Alzheimer's disease could be diagnosed before the patient dies.

Similarities were noted during autopsy between the brain structures of very old people and younger individuals with Alzheimer's or presenile dementia. Blessed and associates[32] counted the number of senile plaques and neurofibrillary tangles

---

[30] RN. Butler, Myrna I. Lewis, Aging and Mental Health, C.V. Mosby Co., New York, 1977: 88

[31] The Associated Press, January 10, 2002

[32] G. Blessed, B.E. Tomlinson and M. Roth, The Association between Quantitative Measures of Dementia and of Senile Change in the Cerebral Grey Matter of Elderly Subjects, British Journal of Psychiatry 114 (1968): 797-811

and as a result, the distinction between presenile and senile dementia was dropped. Soon afterward, both categories were referred to as Alzheimer's. The name became synonymous with senility and almost overnight it became a common illness. In the new edition of their book *The Vanishing Mind,* Heston and White[33] describe the new situation as follows: "Alzheimer's disease and senile dementia are now regarded as one disease. And over the last few years, both terms have been discarded in formal communication in favor of dementia of the Alzheimer type (DAT), or, senile dementia of the Alzheimer type (SDAT). Pending discovery of evidence to the contrary, we assume the basic disease process is the same, regardless of age at onset."

A comparison of the DSM and ICD guidelines on Dementia and Alzheimer's Disease

The newly released *DSM-V* takes a totally different approach to dementia diagnoses than the *DSM-IV*. The chapter title is "Major or Mild Neurocognitive Disorder Due to Alzheimer's Disease." It further differentiates between Alzheimer's disease due to hereditary factors or Alzheimer's disease marked by a) clear evidence of decline in memory and learning and at least one other cognitive area, b) steadily progressive, gradual decline in cognition, without extended plateaus, AND c) no evidence of other diseases or neurological, mental or systemic conditions that could contribute to cognitive decline. It also references 'Probable Alzheimer's disease' and 'Possible Alzheimer's disease.' The newest version of the *ICD-10* still lists Alzheimer's disease with early onset and Alzheimer's disease with late onset, as well as 'Other Alzheimer's disease.' The criteria for diagnosis or guidelines include:

- Slow onset, sometimes difficult to pinpoint when it exactly began.

- Progressive decline.

- A significant measure of cognitive deficits, such as memory impairment (both in learning new information and in

---

[33] Leonard L. Heston, June A. White, The Vanishing Mind, W.H. Freeman & Co., New York 1983, 1991

recall), aphasia (language problems), apraxia (inability to use objects or do physical activities), agnosia (inability to recognize objects), loss of 'executive functioning' such as planning, organizing, or having judgment and insight. These losses are severe enough to cause dysfunction in work and social situations.

- There is no other identifiable reason for these symptoms. It is a diagnosis of exclusion.

- In laboratory testing done after death one can see:
  o a significant loss of neurons (nerve cells in the brain),
  o neurofibrillary tangles and amyloid plaques
  o a reduced amount of neurotransmitters.

Early on-set dementia in Alzheimer's disease progresses quickly and has many more symptoms which begin earlier on in the disease process. Late on-set Alzheimer's disease progresses more slowly and is primarily characterized by the symptom of severe memory loss.

The Validation Assessment

In my view, the present attitude is confusing. In the first place, early onset Alzheimer's is a much more distinctive disease than late onset Alzheimer's. In old-old age it is quite normal to get neurofibrillary plaques and tangles in the brain. Nobel Prizewinner Carlton Gajdusek, who discovered plaques and tangles in New Guinea in 1960, wrote in 1987 that these plaques are the hallmarks of old age and that 90% of people over 90 years of age develop them in their brain. Neurologist Dennis Selkoe makes a similar point: "Most of us who live into our late seventies will develop at least a few senile plaques and neurofibrillary tangles, particularly in the hippocampus and other brain regions important for memory," and he adds: "For the most part, the distinction between a normal brain aging and Alzheimer's Disease is quantitative rather than qualitative.[34] It is important to point out that some people whose brains on autopsy show plaques and tangles have led relatively normal lives before dying. Yes, they might have become forgetful, but it is normal for very old people to forget. We begin losing brain cells in our twenties. In fact, German researchers Heiko and Eva Braak did a study of over 800 brains of people of various ages and found 'tangle related lesions' in 20-year-old people.[35] By the time we reach our eighties, there can be significant loss of recent, or short-term memory. This is a normal part of aging, not a disease. The *DSM-IV* clearly supports this:[36] "Dementia must be distinguished from the normal decline in cognitive functioning that occurs with **aging** (as in Age-Related Cognitive Decline) (note: emphasis is in the original document). The diagnosis of dementia is warranted only if there is demonstrable evidence of greater memory and other cognitive impairment than would be expected due to normal aging processes and the symptoms cause impairment in social or occupational functioning."

There is another reason why it is confusing to lump early and late onset Alzheimer's together. The anatomical structures that change the brain and are seen at autopsies are not the sole orchestrators of behavior at very old age. The condition of the brain is rarely the answer to the behavior of the living old person.[37] Scientists who are doing brain research do not work with living old people, they usually study cadavers. The one long-term study that I have seen that attempted to study Alzheimer's disease in the living is the 'Nun Study'. David Snowdon studied 678 Catholic sisters ranging in age from 78 to 106. Clinical information from autopsies performed after their deaths, was compared to behavioral and cognitive changes that were seen over a period of 15 years.[38] He found the following links between 'life factors' and Alzheimer's disease. The higher the level of

[34] Dennis J. Selkoe, Amyloid Protein and Alzheimer's Disease, Scientific American, November 1991

[35] David Snowdon, Aging With Grace, Bantam Books, New York, 2001

[36] DSM-V, see Note 27

[37] See Note 26 - Verwoerdt

[38] David Snowdon, Aging With Grace, Bantam Books, New York, 2001

education, the less chance of developing Alzheimer's disease; the lower the level of education, the more chance of developing AD. This may have to do with the fact that how one uses one's brain in later life plays a role in how much it atrophies. If we continue to develop our brain function we can overcome the damage to brain cells that is a normal part of aging. Snowdon found that a positive attitude towards life, resilience in dealing with difficulties and the expression of emotions are positively correlated with orientation. And lastly, the older one gets, the less likely one is to develop AD. Once nuns had reached their 90's, the percentage that developed AD went significantly down. It is interesting to note that the condition of the brain (size and amount of plaques and tangles) did not always match the condition of the person in life. There were many cases of nuns who had been alert, oriented and 'with it' up until the end, whose brains had severe degeneration; then there were nuns who had become disoriented and withdrawn and had brains that had little degeneration.

His conclusions support my thesis that how a person lives her life is a major factor in late-life disorientation or the development of Alzheimer's disease. The behavior of those with early onset dementia typically follows the Alzheimer's model. Those with late onset dementia are what I call the disoriented old-old. I see these as two very different conditions. The first is a disease process and the second, a reaction to physical deterioration combined with the inability to cope with an overwhelming amount of psychological and social losses.

Differences between patients with Alzheimer's disease and the disoriented old-old:
In hundreds of nursing homes and hospitals I have noticed that patients with early on-set Alzheimer's disease and disoriented old-old have different behavior, speech, gait, and expressions of human needs. Disoriented old-old respond to Validation, communicate better, their speech and gait improve. (See the research studies describing the results of Validation on page 60.) These people can often be helped without medication. Early onset Alzheimer's patients, on the other hand, continue to deteriorate to

the phase of vegetation no matter what method or therapy is used. The course of the disease is progressive regardless of Validation interventions. The behavior of early onset Alzheimer's patients cannot be predicted. Validation may restore some social interaction for a moment, but the next moment the patient may become violent, wander away or withdraw without motivation. Unlike the immediate recognition response of the old-old, the eyes of an early onset Alzheimer's patient usually remain unfocused, blank, staring without recognition. Their gait is often stiff and robot-like. Their facial expressions are not always a reflection of emotions, rather like a mask. Loss of speech occurs quickly in the disease process. One can look at the differences between people with early onset Alzheimer's disease and disoriented old-old in the following ways.

Physical differences: while scientists have found some degree of degeneration in the brains of younger people, it is not normal to have large numbers of plaques and tangles in the brains of 60-70 year old people. Plaques and tangles are found in increasing amounts as people age, independent of the level of orientation.

Psychological differences: 60-70 year old people are not normally preparing for death; they are not in the final life stage. Very old people have entered into the final life struggle. Disoriented very old people are trying to resolve unfinished issues so that they can die in peace. They are in the 'Resolution' stage of life.

Social differences: younger elderly people are usually still engaged in a social network, they have some family, friends and while society does marginalize older people, they are still able to take part in some normal social activities. Disoriented very old people have disengaged from social networks; they have lost the social roles they once had.

Validation Workers

Disoriented old-old have different life goals than their caregivers. This section describes the attitudes and qualities that are needed in order to practice Validation effectively. The techniques are secondary. Most importantly, the Validation worker must accept that the disoriented old person's withdrawal inward can be a normal part of aging, their return to the past is a survival method, a healing process and a way of easing the blows dealt by aging. Old age is not a disease. The Validation worker accepts the physical deterioration of very old people and knows that their life goals differ from those of young, healthy individuals.

Goals for Younger Individuals

- Think. Produce. Use your head. Figure things out.
- Communicate clearly. Use well-chosen dictionary words.
- Keep track of clock-time. Avoid daydreaming.
- Control your emotions.
- Confine wishful thinking to coffee breaks, dreams, holidays.
- Conform to society's rules.
- Become "somebody." Work to achieve success.

Goals for Disoriented Old-old

- Retreat from painful present day feelings of uselessness.
- Relive past pleasures.
- Relieve boredom by stimulating sensory memories.
- Resolve unfinished conflicts by expressing feelings.

Validation workers, or V/Ws, are non-judgmental; they accept and respect the wisdom of old people. The V/W never walks in front of the old-old trying to convince them of the present. Nor does he or she patronize the old-old by walking behind them, pretending to agree with them. Sure of their own reality, they can afford to walk beside the mal– and disoriented. V/Ws are always honest. Disoriented old-old people recognize pretense. The deaf will "hear" a snicker. The blind will "see" a smirk. They know the difference between the put down pat and warm, respectful human contact. On a subliminal level of awareness the old-old know the truth, like a sleeper who unconsciously swats a mosquito, they are unaware and do not want to be made aware. Therefore, the V/W never lies. The disoriented old-old do not trust the worker who lies. Without trust, validation cannot work.

The V/Ws mission is to help the disoriented old-old accomplish their final life task: to die in peace. To do that the disoriented old-old need to be heard by a trusted listener who respects the feelings of old people, and knows that each feeling is genuine. Imprisoned emotions demand to be released in this quest for resolution; to see the light of day during this final life stage. The V/W knows that when human feelings are acknowledged and validated, the old-old disoriented feel better. Their stress is relieved. Listening does not "feed the fantasy." Listening with empathy reduces anxiety.

The disoriented old-old person is not a child. The V/W is not a parent and does not use "parent" words, such as "should," or "must?"[39] The V/W does not punish, threaten or patronize. Workers do not shut off the old person's feelings nor force expression of feelings, respectful of disoriented old-old's privacy. V/Ws tune into their client; pick up rhythms; listen to verbal clues; and observe non-verbal clues. The V/W puts feelings into words to affirm them and to give dignity to the very old person. Validation means respecting the disoriented old-old who have lived a lifetime and acknowledging their wisdom. V/Ws do not expect all disoriented old-old to act alike, but respect the unique differences in all people.

The Validation Worker uses empathy. We do not judge three year-olds by our adult standards. All of us have been three years old and can step into their shoes. We do not call teenagers psychotic when they act out their feelings. All of us have been

---

[39] Thomas Harris, I'm OK, You're OK, Harper & Row, New York, 1967

teenagers and know that they are in a stage of rebellion, trying to find their own identity.

None of us, however, have been old-old. It's much harder to step into the wheelchair of a 90-year-old man who pounds his fist, cannot see clearly, hear well, move or remember his name, and certainly not ours. It's much harder to move to his rhythms and see with his eyes. He cannot see his hand. He sees a hammer and a nail. This old man was an expert carpenter; his father and grandfather were also carpenters. He learned to pound a nail straight as a child. As an old man he sits and pounds to restore his identity. The Validation worker has empathy for him. We can step into the lives of the old-old, because we too have suffered losses.

Have you ever felt the momentary panic of losing your bearings when driving alone at night in a storm, with no one to ask directions? Then you've felt the bewilderment of the disoriented old-old who forget where they are. Have you experienced numbness of a limb, blurry vision, impaired hearing, felt the loss of someone or something you loved, the anxiety of losing a job, a home, a physical capacity? If you have felt generalized fear, rage, jealousy, guilt, grief, and love, then you can share human feelings with disoriented old-old.

The Validation Worker is a super-adult who has achieved adult intimacy, identity, has separated from authority and is able to express herself without fear of rejection. V/Ws are responsible for their own feelings even when they are uncomfortable. They can accept raw, gut emotions from disoriented old-old and mirror them with empathy. When an old woman rocks, crying, "a ma ma ma," the V/W acknowledges the old woman's need for her mother, using the appropriate Validation techniques. There is genuine eye contact between the V/W and the disoriented old-old woman, who no longer turns to the past to find love. She has found it with the V/W.

Care-givers who cannot share intimate feelings with disoriented very old people who freely express them, should not be working with them. People who communicate only on verbal, intellectual, controlled, logical levels will be unable to use the

Validation techniques with empathy. They will be very uncomfortable, will turn away from the disoriented old-old or sedate them. Not everyone should do Validation. Workers who cannot accept strong emotions can work well with oriented and maloriented very old people who do control their feelings.

Validation workers are superhuman for 3-10 minutes, because they can empathize with very old disoriented people, and respect their feelings as valid, without knowing why the old person acts that way. Super-adult V/Ws do not expect the entire nursing home staff to practice Validation. They respect the fact that some staff may not be able to cross the street to walk in the footsteps of the disoriented old-old. Some staff members expect the older person to do the crossing, to be aware of present day reality. The wise old person will ignore this staff member saying to himself, "I wait for the one that doesn't argue with me."

The Validation Worker is not an Analyst.

The V/W knows that the old-old disoriented have lost the cognitive capacity for insight. They can no longer relate their emotions to intellect or "figure out" the reasons behind their feelings in order to change their behavior. They have lost the capacity for the "AHA!" the sudden realization. With empathy, the V/W sees with the eyes, hears with the ears, and mirrors the body rhythms of the old-old people, in order to help them meet their need for identity, love, and validation of their raw emotions.

The V/W knows that the disoriented old-old usually will **not completely resolve their unfinished life tasks. They will be resolving them until they die.** They can never achieve sufficient insight to completely change their behavior. They need a nurturing, validating person who respects their feelings, listens, affirms, and walks beside them on the streets of the past.

Burn Out and Feelings of Failure[40]

Feelings of failure occur when workers expect disoriented old-old people to behave according to the workers' standards: speak

[40] Beth Rubin, Burnout: Causation And Measurement, Unpublished Master's Thesis, Department of Psychology, Michigan State University, East Lansing, Michigan, 1982

clearly, control emotions, make daily progress, obey rules, listen, or communicate with words. If the worker can accept the physical deterioration of the old-old disoriented person she will rarely experience burn out or feelings of failure. Burn out results from unrealistic expectations, when workers forget that the old-old disoriented will not and cannot remember names, the time of day or the date. They will remember a genuine touch, warm eye contact, and a nurturing voice-tone. Their eyes will light, they smile for the first time in months and the worker feels pleasure in inspiring a life. One moment of genuine sharing makes up for many difficult hours with residents.

Ways to Prevent Burn out:

- have realistic expectations

- set realistic goals for each old-old person

- acknowledge and chart your progress

- get support from wherever you can: family members, staff, volunteers, coworkers

- organize a Validation team

- gain pleasure by listening to disoriented old-old and moving with them

Change comes in small fragments, but it does come. Three months of consistent Validation will bring significant improvements in behavior.[41] Measuring change by using the Validation Evaluation of Progress chart on page 155, will help workers see their progress. Families can participate in Validation by attending regular family workshops. When family and staff share Validation they support each other and everyone enjoys the pleasure of the wisdom, poetry and intimacy that are part of disorientation in old-old age.

In any institution, the administrator's understanding and approval of Validation goals is vital, especially when the V/W begins to form a Validation group. Forming one depends upon the support of the entire staff: housekeeping, dietitians, social

---

[41] Naomi Feil, Group Work with Disoriented Nursing Home Residents, Social Work with Groups 5, No.2 (Summer 1982), Haworth Press, New York: 57

service, nursing personnel and recreation workers. If the administrator and director of nursing do not support Validation, the nursing aide may not be instructed to take each group member to the toilet before the meeting, the meeting room may not be available, and staff members might interrupt and take individuals out of the group, destroying its continuity. Lack of staff support will burn out the V/W who wants to begin a group; however, individual Validation can still be practiced.

A Validation team can include just a few people or as many as an entire institution. Through regular meetings, you can evaluate your progress, share your experiences, express your frustrations and gain insights into your own behavior. A team gives you support and alleviates isolation.

What Validation Can Do

Validation is a process through which disoriented old-old people can communicate, verbally and non-verbally, whatever is in their minds and hearts at that moment. Whether the person is happily working away at a job that he misses, struggling with an unfinished life task or reliving a crisis that never was resolved, the goal of Validation is to meet the client in his reality so that he is not alone.

Disoriented old-old people respond to Validation. Change in behavior is slow and fluctuates from day to day, but permanent change does occur.

These are some of the results that you can expect:
- they sit more erect
- their eyes open
- increased social controls
- less crying, pacing, pounding (repetitive behaviors)
- less anger
- less need for chemical and physical restraints
- increased verbal communication
- increased non-verbal communication

- improved gait
- resolving unfinished life tasks
- reduced anxiety
- increased feelings of well being
- less withdrawal
- a greater sense of self-worth
- the assumption of familiar social roles through Validation groups
- restoration of a sense of humor
- can maintain themselves longer in their own homes

For Caregivers:
- more joy and energy
- reduced stress
- family members communicate more

Results of Research Studies

My study at the Montefiore Home for the Aged in 1971, showed that after five years of Validation, thirty organically brain-damaged, disoriented old-old people improved in many ways. They became less incontinent, there was less negative behavior (crying, pounding, hitting), and more positive behavior (smiling, talking, helping others). People became more aware of external reality; they talked outside of group meetings, and were more content.[42]

In 1976, also at The Montefiore Home for the Aged in Cleveland, I compared four years of transcriptions of two groups. One was the "coffee klatch group," of oriented, very old nursing home residents with physical disabilities. The other was the "Tuesday group" of disoriented, very old residents in the same nursing home. This comparison showed that denial is the common defense against stress for the disoriented old-old who withdraw to the past.[43]

[43] Naomi Fell, A Comparison of Oriented and Disoriented Residents, Unpublished study Montefiore Home, Cleveland, Ohio, 1976

[42] See Note 4

In 1980, Stan Alprin, a Cleveland researcher, took a very different approach to the assessment of Validation. He examined its impact on the therapist's attitude and behavior as well as its effect on the disoriented very old nursing home resident. Alprin obtained quantified data with regard to behavioral changes of residents and staffs in nursing home settings in 16 homes throughout the United States who were using Validation with disoriented very old residents. He surveyed directors, activity personnel and social workers. He reported: "The evidence obtained thus far would suggest very strongly [that there were] many positive changes in behavior of resident groups following Validation...Shifts in staff behavior were in a positive direction."[44] Those shifts included: more trust between nursing staff and residents, less aggressive behavior exhibited by the residents, less staff turnover.

In her Master's thesis for the University of Akron, Ohio, Marlene Peoples compared the effects of Validation with Reality Orientation (RO) in a 225 bed nursing home in 1982. She used standardized statistical tools to assess the degree of confusion in small groups. There were "qualitative improvements in behavior for seven of the ten subjects in the Validation group compared with three of the eight subjects in the Reality Orientation group. Attendance at the Validation group was better. Validation produced significant improvement in behavior...whereas Reality Orientation produced no significant difference."[45] I received other studies that corroborate this finding.

In 1986, Paul A. Fritz, a professor at the University of Toledo, analyzed the effectiveness of Validation on speech patterns of cognitively impaired very old residents of nursing homes in Toledo, Ohio. He wrote: "I found that Validation made a significant improvement on the elders' speech patterns. I used a computer program which measures the number of verbs, nouns, prepositions, etc. that a person uses in recorded conversation. I

---

[44] Stan Alprin, The Study to Determine the Results of Implementing Validation Therapy, Unpublished study, Cleveland State University, September 1980

[45] Marlene Peoples, Validation Therapy Versus Reality Orientation As Treatment for Disoriented Institutionalized Elderly, Unpublished Master's Thesis, College of Nursing, University of Akron, Akron, Ohio, 1982

found that the categories of Malorientation and Time Confusion [two of the four phases of resolution as defined later in this book] showed a significant increase in fluency levels and in lucidness."[46]

James T. Dietch, M.D. of the Irvine Medical Center in California, and others, published their study, "Adverse Effects of Reality Orientation" in 1989. It states: "This validation approach was found to be more effective than application of Reality Orientation...Validation Therapy differs radically from RO and appears to be a useful approach in some patients with dementia... Staff may benefit by avoiding the repetitive frustration of attempting to reorient patients in areas they are incapable of changing. Greater staff awareness of the individual psychological and emotional needs of dementia patients will result in improved therapeutic care."[47]

In Australia, Colin Sharp PhD, research and evaluation consultant compared identical populations in two nursing homes, one used Validation and the other did not. In 1989, he found that both staff and residents benefited from Validation. There was a reduction of withdrawal and more positive interaction and socialization. The efficacy of Validation was manifested in the Validation home.[48] Ian Morton and Christine Bleathman, nurses at Maudsley Hospital in London concur with Sharp's findings in their 1991 study.[49]

In 1991, Dr. Jean Prentczynski, a French physician and researcher, carried out a study similar to Sharp's at the Hospital Sebastopol in Reims, France, with similar results. "There was an increased resolving of their conflicts and reduced anxiety, less suspicion and increased trust with staff"[50]

---

[46] Paul Fritz, The Language of Resolution Among The Old-Old: The Effect of Validation Therapy on Two Levels of Cognitive Confusion, Research results presented to the Speech Communication Association, November 1986, Chicago, Illinois

[47] James T. Dietch, Linda J. Hewett and Sue Jones, Adverse Effects of Reality Orientation, Journal of American Geriatric Society 37 (1989): 974-976

[48] Colin Sharp and Alan Johns, Validation Therapy: an Evaluation of a Program at the South Port Community Nursing Home in Melbourne, Australia, Paper presented at the Australian Association of Voluntary Care Associations, Melbourne, Victoria, Australia, November 10-13, 1991

[49] Ian Morton and Christine Bleathman, Does It Matter Whether It's Tuesday or Friday? Nursing Times 84, No. 6 (London, 1988): 25-27

[50] Jean Prentczynski, Thesis, Department of Medicine, University of Reims, France, December 20 1991

Janet Fine and Susan Rouse-Bane[51] were one of the few research teams that looked at the effects of individual Validation techniques on resident behaviors. Their results were generally positive.

Dr. Frederic Munsch is the first person who has produced a professional based on the correct use of Validation. Dr. Munsch is a psycho-geriatric physician as well as a certified Validation Teacher. In 2000 he published his results: increased communication and less agitation etc. after 9 months of Validation group work[52].

In Finland, (2002) one hundred and twenty two trained Validation caregivers were questioned about the effects of Validation in their work. Validation was seen as being helpful in daily care and especially during difficult moments between patient and staff member. Patients were more active, physically more stable, communicated more and seemed to have more self-confidence[53].

In 2004, Tertianum ZfP in Switzerland, and the German research institute, idea-l, published their study on the effects of professional Validation training on the relationship between caregiver and care recipient. They found that training changed the care-givers behavior in a positive way so that difficult situations were handled more effectively. Caregivers felt more security and understanding. The behavior of care-receivers was improved: less conflicts, a better atmosphere, reduction of medication.

In 2007, Tondi, Ribani, Bottazzi , et al, studied Validation Therapy in a Nursing Home: a case-control study. Nursing home residents were divided into a study and control group. The study group was given both individual and group Validation. After 4 months measurements were taken and the study group was found to have reduced agitation, apathy and irritability. There was a

[51] Janet Ikenn Fine and Susan Rouse-Bane, Using Validation Techniques to Improve Communication with Cognitively Impaired Older Adults, Journal of Gerontological Nursing 21(1995), No.6: 39-45

[52] Frederick Munsch, Prise en Charge des Troubles Psycho-comportementaux Chez des Personnes Agees en Institution, Atteintes de Deficiencies Cognitives, Faculte de Medicine, Universite de Limoges, (2000).

[53] idea-l and Tertianum ZfP, 2004, Evaluationsstudie über die Praxiserfolge von Validation nach Feil am Beispeil eines Tertianum ZfP Validation Anwenderseminars. Retrieved from
https://vfvalidation.org/validation/Gunther_EvaluationsstudieUberDiePrax.pdf

moderate improvement in sleep disorders and feeding dependence.

C. Siviero, E. Mazza, and A. Cerri of the Castellini Foundation in Melegnano, Italy concluded a case study which was presented at a national congress of the Society of Gerontology and Geriatrics in 2009. This study found that the consistent use of Validation by most caregivers on a dementia unit maintained the patient's functional abilities; behavior disorders were significantly reduced; the patient now enjoys good relationships with both the staff and other patients and she is involved in department activities. A number of case studies and anecdotal reports have been published, as well as literature reviews. In all cases Validation was seen as a welcome and useful method. (1996, D. Gagnon; 1996, R. Woods; 1997, E. Grasl; 1997, C. Day; 1998, L. Touzinsky; 1999, B. Benjamin)

All studies and reports on Validation that are given to the Validation Training Institute, are published on the website: www.vfvalidation.org.

Many of the earlier studies done on the effects of Validation have provided only anecdotal or questionable results. The lack of supporting research is one of the greatest criticisms of Validation. However, in recent years the availability of training has increased, there are more instruments to measure the effects that Validation brings about and the development of Validation centers throughout the world has made it more possible to share information and resources. Thousands of persons have been trained to use Validation in homes, nursing facilities, hospitals and communities throughout the world. These practitioners have experienced positive results from its effects and it is hoped that future research will clear the criticism and help people accept Validation.

For more information on Validation research, please see **https://vfvalidation.org/web.php?request=research_on_validation**

A= description of population
B= was group or individual Validation used
C= what was measured

D= results from study
E= was Validation really used

Authors	A	B	C	D	E
Feil 1971, 1976	30 organically brain-damaged, time confused	G	Positive behaviors: attentive, smiling, involved with others, expression of joy/anger without acting out. Negative behaviors: sitting hunched forward, restless, pacing, unable to look at others, uses body movement instead of speech, hits, bangs, scratches or shows apathy.	All except one group member showed an increase in positive affect. 8 group members showed a decrease in negative affect. 11 showed increased interaction and less anxiety.	Yes
Alprin 1980	16 nursing home directors, activities directors or social workers reporting on residents in Time Confusion or Repetitive Motion	?	Global assessment of resident behavior before and after Validation. Global assessment of staff behavior before and after training in Validation.	Reduction of "negative behaviors" and increase in positive behaviors after the introduction of Validation. Positive changes in staff behavior after training.	?
Peoples 1982	29 residents (mean age 87.7) divided into 3 groups: Validation, Reality Orientation and a Control group. Validation group was run for 30 minutes on 5 consecutive days	G	Comparison of Reality Orientation and Validation in restoring orientation, ego integration and behavioral characteristics. Tool for Assessing Degree of Confusion in the Elderly (Hogstel), Ego Integration Scale, Behavior Assessment Tool.	With Validation, significant improvement in behavior but not in orientation or ego integration; with Reality Orientation, no significant difference. Validation produced more qualitative changes in behavior.	?

Authors	A	B	C	D	E
Robb 1986	12 residents in a control group; 9 in an experimental group; 6 in a quasi-experimental group. All were 60 yrs old+, with disorientation not from neurological disease. Mean age 80/81 years old. Validation group was run 2 x weeks for 9 months.	G	Effects of Validation on mental status (Mental Status Questionnaire by Fishback), morale (Philadelphia Geriatric Center Morale Scale by Lawton), social behavior (Minimal Social Behavior Scale by Farina, Arenberg, Guskin.)	No significant change in pre and post testing. Measuring instruments were problematic. The "therapy" was found to be labor intensive and expensive. There was little support or understanding from other staff.	No (Note: it was clear from the description of this study that the group leaders were not trained in Validation.)
Fritz 1986	11 Maloriented and Time Confused residents. 2 sessions/week for 10 weeks.	I	Effect of Validation on use of language and language patterns.	For Maloriented residents: increased use of figurative subjects and objects of verbs, could "name" instead of blame the objects in their environment.	?
Babins 1988	5 disoriented residents	G	Social behavior, verbal interactions, eye contact, touch	More expression of feeling, improved cognitive ability	?

Authors	A	B	C	D	E
Dietch 1989	3 case studies; 2 women (84, 85 years old), 1 man (74 years)	I	Effectiveness of Reality Orientation and Validation Case study presentation	Reality Orientation produced negative responses.	?
Sharp 1989	18 & 19 elderly residents in 2 nursing homes (average age 87.1, 89.7)	I	Phase of resolution, Behavioral Problem checklist, Goal Attainment Scaling	Most made substantial improvements, few deteriorated, the rest remained the same	?
Morton & Bleatlunan 1991	5 elderly residents with dementia	G	Verbal interaction, communication, behaviors	Increased quantity and quality of interaction	?
Prentczynski 1991	3 residents: 83yrs, 88yrs - both disoriented, 70 yrs w/Parkinson	I	Verbal communication eye contact, touch, smiling, "positive affect", takes initiative	Reduced disorientation, less need for medication, improvement in criteria	?
Scanland 1993	34 (avg age 76.8) split in 4 groups: 1 Validation group, 1 Reality Orientation group, 2 control groups	G	Effects of Reality Orientation and Validation on functional status, cognition, level of depression	VT had no effect on mental status or morale, slightly increased depression level	?
Fine & Rouse- Bane 1995	22 residents in "Resolution phase"	I	Staff=s utilization of appropriate technique, the effectiveness of the technique (reduction of problem behaviors)	Improvement of staffs use of Validation techniques - reduction of problem behaviors	?

Authors	A	B	C	D	E
Toseland 1997	88 nursing home residents, (avg age 88) in 4 different facilities, assigned to a Validation Group, a Usual Care control group or a social contact group.	G	Level of dementia, self-care, depression, withdrawal, levels of agitation, levels of positive behavior=, medications	Reduced physical and verbal aggressive behavior, no change in use of medications	?
Munsch 2000	One group of 5, (avg. age 85.8) and one group of 7, (avg age 83) disoriented residents	G	Levels of agitation and levels of positive behavior using the Cohen Mansfield Agitation inventory, Neuropsychiatric Inventory	Improvement on both scales in all cases	Yes
Sipola Lumijärvi 2002	122 caregivers trained in Validation	I	Was Validation useful and/or effective in caregiving? What changes were seen by caregivers?	Validation was seen as being helpful in daily care and especially during difficult moments between patient and staff member. Patients were more active, physically more stable, communicated more and seemed to have more self-confidence	Yes

Authors	A	B	C	D	E
Tertianum Zfp & idea-1 2004	Course participants of a Level 1, Validation Worker course in a nursing home.	I	Does Validation training improve the relationship between caregivers and clients; ex. was there a reduction in conflicts and less use of chemical restraints. Is there more understanding of older, demented people and is there a stronger sense of safety at work?	The course changed behavior of the caregiver in a positive way so that they can better handle difficult situations; they experienced greater safety and more understanding; the behavior of the clients improved; there were less conflicts and a better atmosphere.	Yes
Siviero, Mazza, Cerri (2009)	1 case study	I & G	Effects of Validation using: MMSE, UCLA, CDR and Barthel scales	Improvement on all scales: Functional abilities were maintained; behavior disorders were significantly reduced; patient now enjoys good relationships with both the staff and other patients and she is involved in department activities	Yes
Siviero and Cipriani (2011)	Case study	I & G	Effects of Validation using: MMSE, CDR and NPI	Validation proved to be an effective instrument for the reduction of behavior disorders.	Yes
Siviero, Cerri, Mazza (2012)	Case study	I	Demonstrate the effectiveness of Validation when family members become part of the team		Yes

Coping With Your Own Aging Process

Helen Thomas lives alone. She is 76 years old. When her husband died of cancer three years ago, Helen dried a few tears, shuffled her ambivalent guilt and grief, stomped on her feelings and went on living. She found a volunteer job in a library near her home. Now she shelves books as well as her feelings. She never asks her children for help, never needs help—she thinks. Whenever hardships hit, Helen hits back, never gives in to her fears. She always controls her emotions, always pulls herself together.

It's 5:00 a.m. Helen always wakes up at 5:00 a.m. She opens her eyes - but she can't see. Everything is black. Helen gropes for the night-lamp, turns it on, but there's no light. Did all the fuses blow? Helen blinks away tears and tries to shut down her anxiety. The more she tries to stop the flood of fear, the more she panics. Her heart pounds. Her hands and face are covered with sweat. She feels nauseous. Terror takes over. Helen is blind. She shrieks, "Help! I can't see. Help!" The neighbors call 911. A rescue squad takes her to the emergency room in a nearby hospital. Still screaming, Helen gets the latest tranquilizing medication. Within two weeks, Helen is placed in a nursing home, unaware of the present time or place, her head slumped on her chest in a wheelchair, her eyes closed, hands limp, mouth open, barely breathing—a living dead person.

The diagnosis? Helen is given the standard test to determine her mental status. She cannot count backwards by ten; does not know the name of the President of the United States; can no longer perform simple tasks of daily living; her emotions are labile, spilling out without control; and a CAT scan reveals the possibility of small strokes that have destroyed Helen's brain tissue over the last few years. Diagnosis: "Dementia of the Alzheimer's Type."

How could Helen have prevented her disorientation? With one hundred billion brain cells, and quadrillions of possible connections, a younger Helen could have gained insight, struggled to know herself, to become aware of her pattern of denying unpleasant feelings. She could have developed new ways of coping when hard times hit, but she didn't.

Facing unpleasant feelings is scary. Trying an unknown path is risky. Learning to walk in an unfamiliar direction can lead to panic. We have to be painfully honest with ourselves, risk making mistakes, get used to shame and despair before we can perfect new ways of living. The better we know ourselves, the less likely we are to fall apart in very old age. The more self-aware, the easier it is to cast off worn-out, rusty ways of coping.

Steps for Coping with Aging:

- be honest with yourself, listen to your emotions
- know your preferred sense[54]
- pay attention to your body
- find a coping mechanism for crisis situations
- keep resolving your unfinished life tasks and issues
- accept what you can't change and respect yourself
- accept the physical losses of aging

Here is Helen's life revised. As a girl, she relied on her vision for pure enjoyment of living. She loved painting. Her oil canvases decorated the living room. She used to smear colors, splashing one into the other. When Helen was about 10, she fashioned multicolored dresses for her paper dolls. As a teenager, she would wander in the woods watching the grayish-brown-purple leaves flirt with the wind. Visits to the Art Museum were pure joy. She reveled in the colors of the Dutch Masters. As a mother, Helen dressed herself and her children with care, always matching colors.

As an adult, knowing that seeing is her preferred sense, Helen prepares for aging and possible vision loss by perfecting her other senses. She could take a Yoga class to get in touch with her kinesthetic sense, develop breathing techniques, learn about her body movements, and to cope with internal and external stress.

---

[54] The 'preferred sense' is a concept from Neurolinguistic Programming. In infancy, we are overwhelmed by a battery of sensory information. We are nursing. Our mother feels warm and soft. We taste the sweet milk, hear the sound of her voice, smell her familiar scent, see her lips and her eyes. Too many sensations for a two week-old-infant. To keep our balance, we blot out some of the senses, and concentrate on one. This becomes our preferred sense. As we mature, we use all our senses, but use our preferred sense most of the time, developing and honing it. later in life, we rely on our preferred sense to tell us what is happening in the outside world; to verify our perceptions; to correct any misconceptions we may have about the environment; to adjust our inner reality to what's happening out there.

She could sign up for a dance class to learn how to move with ease, stretch her muscles, stand straight, hold herself together by aligning her body. She should learn what to do in moments of stress, how to survive momentary panic. When she is lost while driving in a strange city, in the middle of the night, with her little boy crying, and no gas station in sight, Helen could overcome her terror. It takes Helen no more than two minutes to follow these:

Steps for Centering:[55]

- Focus on a spot about two inches below the waist. This is your center. The center of your gravity.

- Inhale deeply through the nose, filling your body with the breath.

- Exhale through the mouth.

- Stop all inner dialogue and pay attention to your breathing.

- Mentally follow your breath from your center up in an arc back to your nose.

- Take in the breath and fill your body with it.

- Wash the breath out at the center.

At 50, Helen needs bifocals. She prepares for vision loss by developing her other senses. She takes a class in music. She learns to play the piano, attends more concerts. She refines her sense of taste and smell, studied the art of wine tasting, and becomes a gourmet cook.

At 60, it takes Helen much longer than usual to adjust to the dark. She wonders why her hands get clammy, her eyes narrow, and her heart pounds whenever she is suddenly, unexpectedly faced with the dark. Helen asks her family, at a Thanksgiving dinner, if they remember an incident when she was locked in the dark. Helen's brother chuckles with sadistic glee. When he was five and Helen was four, he locked her in the closet. "You could hear Helen shriek for five blocks." Their mother rescued Helen within

[55] Gay Hendriks and Russel Wills, The Centering Book Prentice-Hall, Englewood Cliffs, NJ, 1975

minutes, but she never forgot the terror of the dark. Her body remembers each detail. Today, at the Thanksgiving meal, her stomach retches at the vivid memory. Similar feelings march through time. A dark movie theater in present time triggers an early memory of being locked in a dark closet fifty years ago. Helen tells her brother how she felt long ago, and how she feels now. In acknowledging her terror of the dark, Helen washes it away. She has added a new insight; a new connection cements in her brain. The "AHA!" brings a "HA-HA!" She feels relief, faces her fears and overcomes them.

At age 63, Helen begins to feel pain in her neck and shoulder. Her body finally rebels, giving her information about herself. In group therapy she realizes that she has always been a martyr. She was a good, little girl, never risking the displeasure of her parents. As a wife, she never said no to her husband and had six children without a murmur. Helen always wanted to go to college, but she had to wait until her youngest child was grown. After years of denial, Helen now consciously changes her ways of responding to others and becomes honest with herself. She learns to say "no" to her husband, her children, and her 90 year old mother, without pangs of guilt or fear of being abandoned. When Helen feels sick to her stomach, or has a pain in her neck, or a tightening in her shoulder, she centers, realigns her muscles, and faces her anger or her fear.

To age successfully:
1. Face each life task as it comes. If you miss a task, go back and tackle it before you reach old-old age. Put your life in order as you go!
2. Learn to play lots of keys on the piano of your life. When one key goes flat, play another. If you begin to go deaf, develop your sense of sight, taste, touch and smell. If your job goes, get involved in volunteer work. Roll with the punches. Expand your coping repertoire while you're young.

Validation in a Nutshell

Disoriented old-old lose controls; lose the will to control; lose their defenses to deny feelings. Their feelings spill without control. In old-old age, they gain the wisdom to freely express feelings in order to resolve them. The Validation worker does not explore feelings that are not expressed. The worker does not analyze feelings that are expressed. Unlike younger neurotic or psychotic patients, disoriented old-old cannot face their feelings. The worker cannot "allow" or "forbid" feelings. Disoriented old-old, with intuitive wisdom of age, will not listen to a younger worker who tells them what to do. They are not children. They will not learn new behaviors. They are summing-up, not growing up. They freely express feelings to resolve them. They are not living to conform to the young worker's expectations of behavior. The worker can modify behaviors of young-old who can return to the community. Old-old will continue to express feelings regardless of the worker. If someone listens genuinely, the feelings often subside. The old person is validated by a trusted listener. The worker never pretends, never forces feelings, never makes fun of feelings or minimizes them through diversion or re-direction.

Principles: are created by Naomi Feil, apply to maloriented and disoriented elderly; they help guide our actions and determine the Validating Attitude.

1. All very old people are unique and worthwhile.
2. Maloriented and disoriented old people should be accepted as they are: we should not try to change them.
3. Listening with empathy builds trust, reduces anxiety and restores dignity.
4. Painful feelings that are expressed, acknowledged and validated by a trusted listener will diminish. Painful feelings that are ignored or suppressed will gain in strength.
5. There is a reason behind the behavior of very old maloriented and disoriented people.

6. The reasons that underlie the behavior of maloriented or disoriented very old people <u>can</u> be one or more of the following basic human needs:
    - Resolution of unfinished issues, in order to die in peace.
    - To live in peace.
    - Need to restore a sense of equilibrium when eyesight, hearing, mobility and memory fail.
    - Need to make sense out of an unbearable reality: to find a place that feels comfortable, where one feels in order or in harmony and where relationships are familiar.
    - Need for recognition, status, identity and self-worth.
    - Need to be useful and productive.
    - Need to be listened to and respected.
    - Need to express feelings and be heard.
    - Need to be loved and to belong: need for human contact.
    - Need to be nurtured, feel safe and secure, rather than immobilized and restrained.
    - Need for sensory stimulation: tactile, visual, auditory, olfactory, gustatory, as well as sexual expression.
    - Need to reduce pain and discomfort.

7. Early learned behaviors return when verbal ability and recent memory fails.
8. Personal symbols used by maloriented or disoriented elderly are people or things (in present time) that represent people, things or concepts from the past that are laden with emotion.
9. Maloriented and disoriented old people live on several levels of awareness, often at the same time.
10. When the 5 senses fail, maloriented and disoriented elderly stimulate and use their 'inner senses'. They see with their 'mind's eye' and hear sounds from the past.
11. Events, emotions, colors, sounds, smells, tastes and images create emotions, which in turn trigger similar emotions experienced in the past. Old people react in present time, the same way they did in the past.

PART TWO: THE PHASES OF RESOLUTION

Maloriented and disoriented old-old have entered the final life stage, Resolution versus Vegetation. They have never achieved what Erikson calls integrity. I have divided this population into four distinct phases. These phases can be identified by their physical and psychological characteristics. Each phase is a further retreat from reality, a slow physical regression. Don't get hardening of the categories, people move from phase to phase sometimes within five minutes. Usually, however, they are in one phase most of the time. A man can be oriented at 8:00 a.m., and at 3:00 p.m. he has to go home to feed his horses and milk the cows.

Phase One: Malorientation – unhappily oriented to reality
Phase Two: Time Confusion – loss of cognitive capacities and 'clock time'
Phase Three: Repetitive Motion – repetitive movements replace speech
Phase Four: Vegetation – total retreat inward

In order to understand the old-old in these four phases, one needs to understand their use of symbols.

Symbols - Tickets to the Past

A symbol is an object or person in the present, that represents a significant object or person from the past.[56] A soft toy can become a mother's hug, a cigarette, the nipple. We all use symbols in art, poetry, and dreams. With our cognitive ability intact, we are able to connect two things or two people, compare them without losing their identity. We can think in metaphors. "My hand is a baby" is a poet's way of comparing two things. The poet knows that the hand is soft like a baby. The hand becomes a symbol of the baby. Maloriented and disoriented old-old also use symbols. The

---

[56] Sigmund Freud, The Basic Writings of Sigmund Freud, vol. I: The Psychopathology of Everyday Life, Random House, New York, 1938: 35-150

maloriented use present-day objects and people to trigger past emotions to express them. A maloriented woman, who has suppressed anger towards her mother, accuses her daughter, who is now her care-giver, "You're neglecting your children. A mother who loves her children doesn't leave them alone with a babysitter." The old woman is thinking of her own mother. She has substituted her daughter for her mother. Disoriented old-old people have lost the cognitive ability to keep objects or people separate. They have lost the "as-if." The hand that feels soft like a baby becomes the baby. The daughter who is the caregiver becomes the old woman's mother. The symbols in both cases refer to people or objects in the past that were real. They did exist.

A symbol can also represent a concept like love, identity, intactness, safety, death, and so forth. A woman in phase three keeps shoe boxes in her nightstand. Through skillful questioning we discover that they represent coffins and the death of her relatives. Another woman packs her handbag with every little thing she can find, napkins, soap, pens, spoons. By filling her handbag with useful items she can hold herself together and in fact says, "Look, I'm all here!" Her bag becomes her identity.

Symbols used by psychotic adults may look like those of a maloriented or disoriented old-old person. Maloriented old-old are frequently diagnosed as having paranoid hallucinations or delusions. A psychotic person fabricates imagined symbols from inner fears. His hallucinations or delusions are pathological, unfounded perceptions of reality and he needs help. His symbols do not relate to the loss of intellectual functioning, nor is he healing himself in a final life stage. Symbols used by disoriented old-old help them heal.

When the outside world blurs because of failing eyesight, diminished hearing and loss of tactile sensations, it becomes easy, and in this final life stage, natural to replace present-day objects and people with the past. Maloriented people often use present-day authority figures (administrator, bus driver, handyman, head nurse, etc.) to express bottled up anger at their parents.

"The administrator never listens to me, he's never around, his door is always closed. When I try to talk to him he's always too busy. But he has time for everyone else." The administrator is a father-symbol. The world of disoriented people has a storehouse of symbols.[57] Neatly, carefully, meticulously, an old-old woman in Phase Two folds, caresses, pats, croons, kissing each fold of a napkin. She is patting herself in place, putting herself in order on this earth. She belongs, is happy. Her world is in order. The napkin enables her to express her longing to be loved, enfolded, warm and safe.

After 45 years of working with maloriented and disoriented people around the world, I have found the following typical symbols.

Universal Symbols and What They Can Mean

A few typical, personal symbols used by disoriented old-old:

A hand	A baby
A finger	A parent, feet to walk, children to walk with
A cloth	Important papers, dough for baking, children's clothes
The arm of a chair	A street
Open space	A hallway at home, heaven, hope
Button, pebble	Nourishment, love
Clucking sound	Safety, joy
Rocking movement	Mother, motherhood, safety, joy
Liquid	Male power
Strong chair	Penis, man, husband, sex
Fork, knife	Anger
Handle	Penis
Low voice	Male person
Spoon or curved object	Woman, female sex
Sock, shoe	Child, dressing a child, or a sexual organ
Removable piece of clothing	Sexual act, freedom, defiance
A nursing home floor	A neighborhood
The hallway	A street in the neighborhood
A wheelchair	A car, bike, carriage

---

[57] Jolande Jacobi, Complex/Achetype/Symbol of C.G. Jung, Princeton/Bollington Edition, Princeton, 1971

I have found these symbols to be universal, regardless of race, religion, culture, or sex. These same symbols are used in Australia, the Netherlands, France, Belgium, Norway, Austria, Canada, Germany, Finland, and the United States.

Phase One: Malorientation

The maloriented hold onto socially prescribed rules with one exception, they need to express past conflicts in disguised forms. They use people in the present as symbols[58] for people from the past: an old-old woman claims her roommate is stealing her underwear. The roommate symbolizes a sister, of whom she was very jealous. A woman who never expressed her sexual desires claims a man is hiding under her bed.

Feelings are denied. Speech, reason and rational thinking are very important. The maloriented person values cool, clear judgment and control, often resenting touch and close eye contact. They keep track of time, think things through, put items into their proper place and keep order. They are ashamed when caught slipping up by occasionally forgetting, repeating a statement or story, or mistaking identities. They confabulate, use made up experiences to cover their gaps in memory, and deny them. Feeling old and useless in an institution or alone at home they sense, this is punishment for past behavior, and say, "Someone is poisoning" their food. Food is a symbol for love. Bitter, alone and unloved they claim, "Someone is stealing" their possessions. They feel robbed by old age and in childhood they felt robbed by sisters, brothers, parents, who "stole" their dignity. Similar feelings march through time, attracting each other like magnets.

To justify themselves or deny their strong emotions as they have throughout their lives, they blame and accuse others. When their partner dies, they never feel grief or guilt, but blame the doctors. They resent retirement, but instead of expressing the anger, they blame the boss for being prejudiced against older people. When they lose their hair due to normal aging, they blame the beautician or barber. To maintain control in a battle against

<hr>

58 See Jacobi Note 57

the loss of controls, they hoard. Fearful of increasing loss, they store up whatever they can - oranges, safety pins, tissues, cups, sugar packets, salt, newspapers, ribbons, to protect themselves against future losses. No one will persuade them otherwise. "Convinced against their will, they hold the same opinion still." The need to justify the past is stronger than "truth." Their deepest fears are projected onto others in order to maintain equilibrium. They need to defend themselves, need their cover-ups. Don't strip them of their defenses, their dignity. They need these types of behavior to survive. Through them they express their feelings without having to expose them to the harsh light of reality. They need a trusting relationship with a nurturing, respectful authority who will not argue with them, who understands and doesn't judge. They need Validation.

Physical Characteristics of Malorientation:

- Eyes are clear and focused.
- Stance is often rigid.
- Movement in space (even in a wheelchair or with a walker) is definite, sustained, precise.
- Face and body muscles are tight.
- Jaw often juts out.
- Fingers and hands are often pointing. The arms often folded.
- Lips are tight.
- Breathing can be shallow.
- Voice tone is clear, often harsh, whining or shrill.[59]
- Often clutch a coat, cane, or purse.
- Cognitive ability is relatively intact, can categorize, have a concept of clock time.
- Can read, write, figure. Use dictionary words.
- Losses to sight, hearing, tactile sensation, mobility are relatively minor.

[59] R Bandler, J. Grinder and V Salk, Changing With Families, Science and Behavior Books, Palo Alto, Cal., 1976

Psychological Characteristics of Malorientation:

- Need to express bottled up emotions.
- Hold onto present reality.
- Want to understand and to be understood.
- Play games with rules.
- Are aware of occasional confusion.
- Deny confusion or confabulate (make up stories to fill in memory gaps).
- Hear, see, talk and move fairly well. Listen.
- Resist change.
- Deny feelings (such as loneliness, rage, fear, sexual longings).
- Blame others when losses become great.
- Cannot achieve insight into the reasons behind behavior.
- Want validation from authority: staff, friends, family, doctors, etc.
- Get furious at others who cannot or will not use self-control.
- Resent touch and intimacy. Do not want their vulnerability exposed.
- Use a "kinesphere", an invisible circle that surrounds every person. Maloriented people feel protected by an inviolable sphere of about 20 inches around the body.

Phase Two: Time Confusion

Too many physical and social losses create the straw that breaks the camel's back. Further loss of eyesight, hearing, mobility, tactile sensation, smell, taste and cognitive capacity make it easy for people to retreat. Time-confused people no longer deny their losses; no longer hang onto reality. They give up trying to hold onto chronological order and retreat inward. They can no longer separate measurements of time. They cannot classify seconds, minutes, hours, days, months or years. They go by inner life-time. Instead of tracking minutes, they track memories. They lose track of present time and trace their lifetime. One feeling triggers another. A person or object in the present is the symbol - the ticket to yesterday. A familiar movement is the transportation vehicle. Vivid images supply the horsepower. Blurry hearing and eyesight, and damaged recent memory are reasons for the trip. Uselessness and loneliness spur them to the past. Feelings of futility are too high a price for awareness of present reality.

Brain damage affects the control centers. Time-confused people lose: adult controls, communications skills, social skills, no longer conform to dress codes or social rules. They miss stimulation from others because they are frequently ignored or isolated. They become incontinent physically as well as emotionally.

In time confusion, the disoriented old-old person returns to basic, universal feelings: love, hate, fear of separation, and struggle for identity. These emotions are expressed by all the disoriented old-old people in hundreds of nursing homes all over the world. Universal feelings are the heart of fairy tales, classics, folk tales, and myths.[60] The Validation worker can empathize with the helpless rage of sleeping beauties who have suffered the sting of the tranquilizing needle, drug, or restraint. The V/W understands their fear of separation, shouts for identity, and wailing for help when they face the unknown. The care-giver acknowledges the universal fear of the dark and death, the longing for belonging, for meaning, for love. Validation workers do not dismiss the cries of disoriented old-old people with, "They only want attention."

A maloriented person becomes time-confused after an onslaught of losses. Had the maloriented been validated, they might not have retreated. Validation would have kept them communicating, expressing and resolving despite their increasing losses. For example: a maloriented man is moved into a nursing home when his son can no longer tolerate his father's accusing, blaming behavior. The move leads to a sudden withdrawal into time confusion. With Validation, his fears could have been expressed when he was still maloriented. The man needn't have been placed in a nursing home or become time-confused. He could have remained in his own home despite his accusations, which would have decreased with Validation.

[60] M. L von Franz, J. Hillman, Jung's Typology, Spring Publications, Zürich, 1975

Physical Characteristics of Time Confusion:

- Muscles are loose. Graceful movements.

- Eyes are clear, but often unfocused, gazing into the distance.

- Breath is slow, sustained.

- Movement in space is slow, indirect, and often questioning: Which way?

- Speech is slow.

- Hand gestures match the feelings, often questioning.

- Voice tone is low and even, seldom whiny or harsh.

- Shoulders tend to slump forward, neck down. The person often shuffles when walking.

Psychological Characteristics of Time Confusion:

- Reality is blurred because of increased deterioration of rational thinking, eyesight and hearing.

- Capable of expressing emotions, but do not remember facts.

- Metaphoric thinking is lost. They do not put people or objects in accepted categories, cannot compare.

- A lifetime of experience has given them crystallized wisdom; they return to an intuitive knowing.[61]

- Know who is genuine and who pretends.

- Remember sensory, pleasurable feelings from childhood.

- Do NOT listen to people in the present.

- Forget recent events, but have excellent recall for past events that hold strong feelings.

- The energy focus is to resolve past unfinished conflicts, to trigger feelings of usefulness and pleasure.

- Use unique word forms from early memories, are poetic and creative. See the "Symofile" story on page 40.

[61] See Note 49

- Cannot play games with rules (such as Bingo).

- Tell time by personal feelings, not by the clock. Time is measured by lifetime experiences.

    Example: A person is hungry for love. Love = food. She demands food right after lunch.

- Use pronouns without specific references. "He" can refer to God, father, devil, self-identity, the world, authority, masculinity, etc.

- There is an increasing use of symbols to represent people and events remembered from the past. They think in (eidetic) images, rather than words.

- Respond to nurturing touch and eye contact with decreased stress.

- Often lose the ability to sing on key.

- Often retain the ability to read, but lose the ability to write.

- Have a short attention span.

- Hear sounds clearly from the distant past, especially when they are deaf.

- Lose adult controls, often demanding immediate satisfaction of instincts such as sex, love and food.

Phase Three: Repetitive Motion

Individuals in Phase Two, who cannot resolve their feelings by sharing them with another person who validates them, often retreat to basic pre-language movements and sounds to nurture themselves and to work through unfinished conflicts from earlier times. Body parts become symbols and movements replace words in this phase of resolution. A person, who feels tied up, dresses and undresses repeatedly to feel free. One who feels emotionally hungry eats chalk to relieve the longing. Others who are angry, pound until their fury decreases.

Each person has a different concept of which feelings are "bad", depending on their parents' concept of "bad" behavior. In old-old age, they have the wisdom to express these feelings to resolve the conflict. Shame, guilt, sexual desire or anger lie buried for a lifetime, hidden, safely controlled. Decades later, in disoriented old-old age, they come to the surface again. A man in Phase Three drops his pants. He wants to prove he is virile for the first time in his life. Or, he finally expresses rage at parents who punished his sexuality when he was an adolescent.

Feelings that have been stopped up for a lifetime now overflow. The plug is gone. Anger at rigid rules, shame for having "messed up" during toilet training, guilt for not performing at the right time in the right place for the right person, are expressed in agitated motion before they cross the finish line.

In Phase Three, speech becomes non-intellectual; a function of the sensory pleasure of tongue, teeth, and lips making sounds. "When logical, secondary-learned speech goes, they return to 'primal linguistic patterns.'"[62] [63] Alone, isolated, wanting their mother, they bring her back by making well-established sounds from their early childhood, "Ma ma ma ma." The movement of the lips smacking together becomes mother. The person is no longer alone; he has brought back his mother as the infant does when it first learns to speak.

Body movement can transport some people into the past. An old-old woman rocks because it triggers the memory of being rocked by her mother. The nurse touching the old woman gently symbolizes mother. The touch becomes the mother's touch, relieving anxiety and restoring safety. With one touch, the woman travels back in time 80 years. A woman in Phase Three uses a sock to represent her son because she used to wash her son's socks. She is going home in her imagination. The sock reminds her of her son, the sock becomes her son.

With vivid images,[64] they change a nursing home into a productive work place and travel to the past. A chair that feels

---

[62] PK. Saha in: Edward Feil, The More We Get Together, film (Cleveland, Ohio: Edward Feil Productions, 1988)
[63] See Fell and Flynn Note 16
[64] Adelaide Biy, Visualization, Barnes and Noble Books, New York, 1979

strong, like a father, becomes "Daddy," an old woman's hand becomes her baby. Individuals who look or sound like friends, relatives or colleagues from the past, become those people, regardless of age or sex. Having lost awareness of their body in space and using vivid memories, these people "walk" or "dance" in their wheelchairs without moving their feet. With careful, familiar hand movements they pantomime, filling in the missing things or people with vivid memory. In all parts of the world, I have found that disoriented old-old use symbols and movements to travel to the past. In Casper, Wyoming a man uses his fingers to drill oil; in Northern Minnesota they chop trees; in farming areas they milk imaginary cows, skillfully moving fingers and hands to recreate the memory. They work in old-old age as they worked for a lifetime. Now they work to survive the bleak present.

Awareness of painful reality causes further retreat into the past. Drugs and restraints often increase withdrawal. Validation through confirmation and sharing feelings in a nurturing relationship often keeps Phase Two from progressing to Phase Three. Validation gives a person in time confusion, moments of rational thinking. It relieves stress and the need to return to the past.

Physical Characteristics of Repetitive Motion:

- Sway or dance.
- Sing but cannot talk in sentences.
- Make humming, clucking, moaning sounds.
- Muscles are loose, move gracefully, but are unaware of movements.
- Are incontinent.
- Eyes are often closed or not focused.
- Cry frequently.
- Fingers and hands pound, beat, tap, button and unbutton.
- Pace.
- Repeat one sound and/or movement over and over.

- Breathing is steady, rhythmic and even.

- Voice is low, melodic.

- Have moments of super physical strength when grasping for love or expressing anger.

- Are ambidextrous when freeing self of restraints.

- Cannot read or write.

- Can sing an early learned song from beginning to end.

Psychological Characteristics of Repetitive Motion:

- Need for speech is lost through disuse.

- Constant movement keep people alive, give pleasure, control anxiety, relieve boredom and confirm existence.

- Ability to think is lost.

- Repetitive sounds stimulate, reassure and help resolve feelings.

- If motivated, can restore well-established social roles.

- Have increasing loss of self-awareness and loss of awareness of their body in space (kinesthetic).

- Unless motivated, shut out external stimuli.

- Have energy for dancing and singing, but much less for talking or thinking.

- Have a short attention span. Cannot focus on more than one person or object at a time.

- Do not respond unless stimulated through a combination of close contact, nurturing touch, voice tone, and eye contact.

- Resigned to isolation and self-stimulation.

- Have the wisdom to try to resolve unfinished conflicts through movement.

- Remember early experiences.

- Can restore some dormant speech and a limited amount of rational thinking. Interact with others, but only in a loving, validating, genuine relationship.

- Cannot play games with rules. Are impatient. Want immediate satisfaction of needs.

Phase Four: Vegetation

In vegetation, the old-old person shuts out the world completely, gives up the struggle to resolve living. Self-stimulation is minimal, enough to survive. When the person in Phase Three is tranquilized, restrained or reality oriented, they often retreat to vegetation. The withdrawal is complete.

I have recorded some evidence of response to validation with disoriented old-old in vegetation. Many Validation Workers report some non-verbal responses. One woman's eyes opened and she called her son's name after three months of continual validation.

People in vegetation need touch, recognition and nurturing as long as they live. In helping the disoriented old-old in earlier phases, the worker may prevent movement to the final phase.

Physical Characteristics of Vegetation:

- Eyes are mostly closed or not focused, blank.

- Muscles loose.

- Sit slumped in a chair or lie in bed in a fetal position.

- Have lost awareness of their body.

- Movements are barely perceptible.

Psychological Characteristics of Vegetation:

- Do not recognize close relatives.

- Rarely express feelings of any kind.

- Do not initiate any activity.

- There is no way of knowing if they are resolving.

PART THREE:
IMPLEMENTING INDIVIDUAL VALIDATION

Three Steps

Step 1: Gather information

In order to practice Validation, the workers must know the people with whom they are working. That means knowing their past, present and future expectations. This assessment also gives the worker a baseline knowledge for evaluating progress. The "History and Baseline Behavior" form on page 154, will help you record the information you need to practice Validation. The "Individual Validation Session Summary" form on page 155 helps to evaluate progress after your validation sessions. You will want to learn the following:

- Phase of resolution.

- Unfinished life tasks, emotions that have not been expressed.

- Unfulfilled basic human needs (see page 21).

- Past relationships i.e.: family, friends, authority figures, death of significant others, children, partner, siblings.

- Jobs, hobbies, unfulfilled ambitions.

- Importance of religion.

- Ways of facing crises.

- How did the person face old age losses?

- Medical history - ask the person directly, read the medical records. Review the psychiatric history for any indication of mental illness in early life.

There are three ways of gathering this information: taking a verbal history, observing the physical characteristics and asking relatives. Because old-old maloriented and disoriented people change, often dramatically throughout the day, the worker must gather information over a period of at least two weeks, meeting with the old person at different times of the day.

History-taking leads to a meaningful relationship. The more you know about a person, the easier it is to use the Validation techniques. You will build trust, which leads to feelings of safety for the disoriented old person. When people feel safe, they gain strength: interactions increase, people begin to speak, they share thoughts and feelings, heightening their self-esteem and sense of dignity. If the person is verbal, ask both "Here and Now" and "There and Then" questions when you take the history. Phrase your questions carefully to avoid raising the old person's anxiety. The maloriented may forget important dates; don't ask questions that refer to specific lengths of time.

"Here and Now" questions:

1. Have you been in this home (hospital, day care center) a long time? (Rather than, "How long have you been in this home?")
2. How do you like the food? The staff? The medical care? Your roommate?
3. Is there enough to do here?
4. Have you been sick since you got here?
5. Are there a lot of activities?
6. What are the other people like? Are they friendly?
7. What brought you here?
8. Are you ever lonely?
9. Is your bed comfortable? Can you sleep at night?
10. Does your roommate make noises at night that disturbs you? What do you do about that?
11. Does it ever bother you when you can't remember a name or a date right away? What do you do then?

The following reactions are typical responses and can help you determine which phase the person is in, most of the time.

The Oriented, integrated old person will usually respond:

V/W: Have you lived here a long time?

Oriented-88-year-old: More than three years. It takes time to get used to the place, but now I like it fine. It's not like my own home....

If the person is maloriented, he will be aware of the present, but will complain about present day circumstances and will avoid answering questions that refer to feelings:

V/W:	Have you lived here a long time?
Maloriented man:	Too long. Every minute is too long. This place smells so bad, it's disgusting. They've never heard of deodorants here. But what can you do with these old people. It's a shame.

If the person is verbal but time-confused, she will not respond to Here and Now Questions. They will instead refer to their former home, their parents, siblings, or jobs:

V/W: Have you been here a long time?
85-year-old-time-confused woman:

> This is my home. I live here. I take care of my sister. My mother is outside.

The person in repetitive motion will not answer with dictionary words, but will blend sounds to form unique words:

V/W: Have you lived here a long time?
92-year-old-Woman in repetitive motion:

> The sums of the somms stick to the senses and I can't get them to fit the allfalls.

"There and Then" questions:
1. Have you been sick a lot during your life?
2. What brought you to the home (day care center, etc.)?
3. Before you came here, were you living in your own home or with your family?
4. Were you born in this country? Was it hard to move?
5. When your wife (husband) got sick, how did you manage? Did your children help?
6. Did you have children? Brothers and sisters?

7. What work did your spouse do? What work did you do?
8. Was your father born in this country? What was his work?
9. Did your mother work?
10. Were you the oldest? The youngest? Did you help take care of your brother(s) or sister(s)?
11. Were your parents strict?
12. What did you do to have fun? Did you like to cook? To dance? Did you sing in Church? Did you go out a lot, or did you like to stay home?
13. Did you travel to other countries? (Mention specific countries to give alternative choices.)
14. Did you have a good marriage? Was he/she with you when you needed them?
15. What did you do to survive hard times?
16. What was the hardest time in your life? The worst time? The best time?

Questions 4, 5, 10, 11, 14, 15 and 16 refer to coping methods (how a person dealt with difficult situations throughout her life time). Questions 1, 6, 7, 12, 13, 14, 16 explore unfinished life issues.

Often the person may not remember the name of a specific country, or song title. A general question such as, "What song do you like to sing?" can raise anxiety. The more specific a question, the easier it is for the older person to answer. A question that contains the answer gives dignity without anxiety. For example, "Do you like to sing Church songs like, Jesus Loves Me, or Hatikvah, or Onward Christian Soldiers?" "Did you travel to France and Germany?" Phrase the question in a way that the old person can pluck the answer. This shows that you have done your homework, you know and understand the person. The person can trust you. You are nurturing and the person feels safe.

If the old person does not remember recent losses and shifts the conversation to his parents and early childhood experiences, he is in Phase Two or Three. Denial of all loss signifies Phase One.

Clear, vivid images of the distant past with little reference to the present means the person is in Phase Two or Three. People in Phase Four will not respond at all or maintain eye contact with the worker.

Observing the person's physical characteristics is another important way of gathering information. Physical characteristics become a summary of how old people have lived their lives. Wrinkles etched in their faces track their coping methods. An old woman with deep smile lines curving from her nostrils to the corners of her mouth, often smiles to cover anger. Rows of furrows in an old man's forehead can show a lifetime of worry. An old man with his shoulders hunched to his ears is defending himself from the outside world. Quick, jerky movements from one place to another reflect an inward panic, "Which way should I go? What do I do now?" Wandering, slow, dream-like movements and eyes that are not focused on anything, often mean a retreat to the past.

Begin your non-verbal assessment with the top of the body and carefully work your way down to the feet. Notice their hair. If their hair is carefully combed, either:

- They are oriented and able to perform activities of daily living;
- They are economically able to afford special care;
- They are maloriented and very concerned with maintaining their outward appearance;
- Their family visits often and is concerned about their appearance.

If their hair is not combed, it could mean that:

- They are aggressive and no one wants to help them;
- They have poor family relations;
- They cannot afford special help;
- They constantly mess up their hair.

Continue down to the face. Look at their eyes. Neurolinguistic Programmers have identified the following physical characteristics and their meanings.[65]

65 R Bandler, J. Grinder, Frogs into Princes, Real People Press, Salt Lake Qty, Utah, 1979

Movement	Meaning
Eyes looking up and to the right	The person is visualizing something
Eyes straight ahead	The person is hearing something
Eyes looking down	The person is feeling something
Rapid breathing	The person is visual
Even breathing	The person is auditory
Deep breathing	The person is kinesthetic
High voice tone	The person is visual
Moderate voice tone	The person is auditory
Low voice tone	The person is kinesthetic

From infancy on, we are developing our preferred sense. See page 70. Of our senses–hearing, seeing, feeling, tasting and smelling–it is the one we use most. In old age, we rely on this preferred sense to create our perception of the world. If this sense is damaged through the natural aging process, we especially suffer. For example: a visual woman who loses her hearing can overcome this loss without a blow to her self-esteem. If she loses her sight, she also loses her main connection to the world, her way of perceiving it is lost.

When you are asking your "here and now", or "there and then" questions, notice the spontaneous eye-movements. If you have just asked, "What was the worst day of your life?" and the person looks up, then you know that most likely he or she is visualizing the scene and is a visual person. You will build trust by using visual words. See the sections on Techniques for specific applications of the preferred sense.

Look at the lower lip, the cheeks, the position of the chin, changes in skin color, shoulders, arms, hands, fingers, chest, legs, and feet. Observe the person's movement in space, even if they use a walker or a wheelchair. Don't come to any conclusions at this point. Record your observations throughout the two week period of gathering information.

Step 2: Assess the Phase of Resolution

Match your observations of the physical characteristics and your information from the verbal history with the typical physical and psychological characteristics of the four phases of resolution, listed in the Part Two. Remember, people change throughout the day. Knowing the phase will help you choose the appropriate Validation techniques to use.

Step 3: Meet with the Person Regularly, Use Validation Techniques

Fill out the Individual Validation Session Summary (page 155). The length of time that one works with an individual (contact time) depends upon the person's verbal capacity, attention span, and the amount of time that a worker has available. With maloriented people, contact time should be between 5 and 15 minutes. Contact with Phase Two can be between 2 and 10 minutes. Contact time with Phases Three and Four should be limited to 1-10 minutes. It's quality, not quantity time that counts. If the worker is available, and the person receptive, use more time. If the old person is in a long-term care facility, interactions should take place at least three times a week; more frequently, for example three times a day, if the person is in an acute-care facility. Interactions can be less frequent if you are working with someone in an out-patient situation, such as at home or in a day-care center. No matter how frequently or infrequently you meet, you must always come back when you have said you would.

Close the interview/interaction when you see any one of the following visible signs of anxiety reduction: with a person in Phase One, the voice is less harsh; the breathing is even; the pulse is normal; the pupils are no longer dilated; the lower lip is relaxed; or the person is smiling. With a person in Phase Two, after you have achieved a moment of intimacy; the person responds with words; speech improves; gait improves; after you have helped the person to interact with others and he no longer needs you. With a person in Phase Three, the repetitive behavior decreases; you have made intimate contact; the negative acting out turns to music, movement or some other form of expression that meets his needs. With persons in Phase Four, after three minutes regardless of the reaction.

Validation can take place anywhere. The housekeeper in a nursing home can validate while she's tidying the room; the nursing assistant, while she is taking the old person to the toilet; the nurse, as she's giving medication; the electrician, while he's changing the light bulbs; the gardener while he's mowing the grass; the family member while he or she is visiting. The only consideration is privacy. There must be a one-to-one relationship that is built on trust, created in a private environment. The 'session' can take place in a large room with other people, but you must create an intimate space, safe from critical comments or anxiety provoking intrusions.

In all cases, the Validation worker must:

- be centered (see page 71)
- observe physical characteristics (eyes, muscles, chin, voice-tone, movement, etc.)
- listen with energy
- not argue the "truth" of facts
- not be judgmental
- be aware of each person's private space, both physically and psychologically

The following techniques are ways to begin a relationship. There is no single formula because every person is different. Each worker must tap his ability to empathize with disoriented old-old. The worker who is honest, genuine, and caring cannot hurt the disoriented old-old person. The wise old person will forgive you if you make a mistake.

Techniques for Phase One: Malorientation

- **Center yourself.** (See page 71) Maloriented people are often hurtful and mean. They turn away friends and family. The Validation worker acknowledges the hurt, puts it in the closet, and tunes into the world of the maloriented. Later, you can express your feelings in your Validation team meeting. (See pages 56 and 57 on Teams.)

- **Use "who, what, where, when, how" questions to explore**. Be a reporter. Explore facts. Avoid feelings. Validate feelings only when the person expresses them. Never ask "why", maloriented people won't know why and it asks for an intellectual answer.

- **Rephrase**. Repeat the gist of what the person has said using their key words, i.e. the words that she emphasizes or accentuates by changing pitch, which indicates an emotional undertone. Pick up her rhythms and mirror the shape of the lower lip (is it tense, curved upward in a smile, pursed, etc.)

- **Use their preferred sense**. Visual words: notice, imagine, picture, remind. Hearing words: hear, listen, loud, sounds like, clear. Kinesthetic words and phrases: feels like, sense, I'm in touch with, that grabs me, strikes me, hits me, that hurts.

- **Use polarity**, ask the extreme:

  o Resident: They steal my underwear.
  o Worker: How often? How much do they take?

  o Resident: It hurts.
  o Worker: How bad is the pain? When is it the worst?

  o Resident: I had a good husband.
  o Worker: What did you love the most about him?

- **Help the person imagine what would happen if the opposite were true.**

  o Resident: They poison my food.
  o Worker: Is there any time that they don't poison it?

  o Resident: There's a man under my bed.
  o Worker: Is there any time that he's not there?

- **Reminiscing**. Exploring the past is good for the soul and stimulates a pleasurable relationship. People in phase one can separate the past from the present. Often unhappy in old age, they can sometimes express their emotions through talking about the past. You can kindle trust when you slowly build the relationship, not ask too many questions at a time and always respect the boundaries of the client.

  o "What happened when you finished school?"
  o "How did you meet your husband (wife)?"
  o "Do you remember childbirth? What happened?"
  o "What was the hardest thing to bear after your mother died?"

- **Help the person find a familiar coping skill**. Using a variation of reminiscence, the V/W can stimulate memories of past situations in which the old person used coping skills that could also help him survive present-day difficulties. Words like "always" and "never" can trigger memories of former ways of dealing with hard times.

  o Resident: I can't sleep at night.
  o Worker: Did this always happen? Did you have this problem when you lived with your husband?
  o Resident: Well he did snore something awful, but he didn't get up and go to the toilet every two minutes, like the old woman I have to live with.
  o Worker: How did you get to sleep when your husband snored so loudly?
  o Resident: I found a sleep tape and played it softly on my tape recorder. He didn't mind. It never woke him up.

People in Phase One retreat from close, intimate relationships and are threatened by feelings. A handshake, a gentle touch on the forearm is enough intimacy for the maloriented. Hugs are often embarrassing and too close for comfort. Tune into the person's need for touch, not your own. Be aware of their need to defend themselves. However, once intimacy is established, some maloriented people want to be touched. Follow their lead.

When to leave:

Before you leave, honestly express your caring and give the maloriented person a respectful handshake. Leave when the anxiety is reduced: breathing is even, voice is level, muscles are relaxed and the eyes are calm (between 5 and 15 minutes of Validation.) Remember that many fear rejection. Say when you are coming back and return on time. If you have been working with someone within a facility and are leaving the facility, ask a team member to replace you. Maloriented people do not form new relationships easily; give them at least two weeks to grieve, reminisce and help them to relate to your replacement.

Example of Validation in Phase One

Characters:	Mr. Frank, age 96, a new resident in a nursing home. Worker, age 52, a nurse trained in Validation
Place:	the nursing station
Time:	10:30 a.m., prime time for high energy, ability to think clearly
Goal:	Build a trusting relationship. Help Mr. Frank survive the crisis of leaving the community to come live in a nursing home. Help him in his struggle to express bottled up anger and hurt.
Medical:	Mr. Frank had a slight stroke 10 years ago. He suffers from Paget's Disease of the knee. He recently had a prostate operation. He has poor vision; otherwise he's in good physical condition. His psychiatric diagnosis is: "SDAT" (Senile Dementia of the Alzheimer's Type) with paranoid delusions.
Social:	His niece reports that: Mr. Frank's parents were very strict; he was divorced; has no close friends; his father told him he was "no good" and he didn't do well at school as a child. He made a fair living as a tailor. His hobby is walking. After his prostate operation he blamed the surgeon for castrating him and he seems angry at all authority.

Worker's Observation of Physical Characteristics:

He sits stiffly, his jaw juts out, eyes are narrowed, cheek muscles and lower lip are tight, and breathing is deep. His hands clutch his cane as if to protect himself and will not let anyone take it, even when he is eating. He speaks in a low, harsh, accusing voice. When asked a direct question he looks down. The veins in his neck protrude when he is angry. His movements in space are quick, tight, jerky and direct.

Evaluation: There are signs of Phase One: denial, blaming, occasional disorientation. His repeated expression of rage at male authorities indicates his need to resolve angry feelings that have been bottled up. His cane seems to represent potency. His preferred sense is kinesthetic. His unfinished life task is rebellion. Because he has never achieved intimacy with anyone, it will be difficult to establish trust. He needs structured, consistent Validation, for 10 to 15 minutes at least once each day.

Validation Interaction:

The worker does not threaten Mr. Frank with feeling words. She uses a respectful matter-of-fact voice-tone, shakes hands and stays outside Mr. Frank's 20 inch private space. She meets his eyes only for a moment and does not probe with words or eyes. She calls Mr. Frank by his last name, respecting his age and experience. She never looks down on him, but sits next to him on an equal plane. She never argues, even though his facts are often "wrong."

Mr. F: That no good goddamn phony. The Herr Doktor. (He spits on the floor in disgust.)

Worker: Who is the Herr Doktor? (Ask open questions)

Mr. F: That s.o.b. hates me. He put manure in my room to make me fall. Dumped garbage all over. Then tore all the pages out of my calendar so I don't even know what holiday is coming up. I can't stand it anymore.

Worker:	He's driving you crazy? (Use the preferred sense, kinesthetic)
Mr. F:	He does it on purpose.
Worker:	You mean he deliberately wants to get you? (Rephrase)
Mr. F:	That's right!
Worker:	Does he do it every day? (Polarity)
Mr. F:	Not only during the day, but at night. Nights are the worst. He doesn't let me sleep. He gives me a roommate who snores and flushes the toilet all the time.
Worker:	(Center–don't laugh) Is there any time when you can sleep through the night? (Imagine the opposite)
Mr. F:	When you're on night duty. But that's only once a month.
Worker:	Was it always this way? (Reminisce)
Mr. F:	When I lived with my niece I could sleep. You remind me of her. She always read me from the bible for a few minutes. And then I could sleep.
Worker	Do you have a bible?

The worker now has a trusting relationship with Mr. Frank because she wasn't confrontational and stepped into his world. She helped him find his own solution to his sleeping problem and helped him to express his anger at authority. After six weeks of one-to-one Validation, for 10 minutes a day, change will occur. His anger will lessen as he expresses it. The worker needs to listen and not judge. He will remain in Phase One with constant validation and not retreat into Phase Two. He will never stop blaming, however. He is always resolving his unfinished life tasks. They will never be resolved. The more adequate he feels, the less he needs to blame the authority, because he no longer feels like a victim.

Techniques for Phase Two: Time Confusion

- **Center** (as previously described)
- **Use "who, what, where, when, how" questions** - never "why" (as previously described)
- **Re-phrase** (as previously described)
- **Use the preferred sense** (as previously described)
- **Polarity, ask the extreme** (as previously described)
- **Help the person imagine what would happen if the opposite were true** (as previously described)
- **Anchored touch.** Move close into the invisible circle that protects us all. Phase Two persons need nurturing and close body contact. They need the stimulus of another human being to reawaken sleeping nerve cells. They have significant loss of vision and hearing and therefore need to be close in order to see and hear another person. Approach the person directly from the front. Approaching from the side may startle them because people in Phase Two have usually lost the ability to see out of the corner of the eye (peripheral vision).

There are two types of touching one can do, general touching and anchored touching. Anchored touching is finding the special places, often on the face, where touch triggers feelings and memories of past relationships. For example, I have found that touching a person with an open hand on the cheek, making slight circles often triggers memories and feelings of 'mother'. General touching is the type of touch we use normally in life, holding a hand, a hand on the shoulder, placing a hand on the knee of the person we are talking with and so forth. In no case should a client be stroked or petted (like a pet) without purpose or energy. Touch is a powerful tool that needs to be used with thought and caring. See the more specific descriptions of anchored touching in the section on using touch with Phase Three individuals.

- **Use genuine, direct, prolonged eye contact.** Touch with your eyes. Bend or sit down if the person is in a wheelchair in order to make direct eye contact.

- **Use a clear, low, warm, loving voice tone.** Harsh tones cause withdrawal or anger. High, weak, soft tones are ignored due to damage to the auditory nerve. Use your diaphragm to project a nurturing clear voice. The voice triggers memories of loved ones. Speak while making eye contact and touching the person in Phase Two, they need the combined stimuli of touch, eye contact and voice in order to respond. Do not speak without touching. Avoid speaking to the person's back, this may raise fear of the unknown.

- **Observe the emotion.** Phase Two persons freely express their feelings. Words begin to fail. The worker must now communicate on an emotional, rather than on a verbal level. A discrete observation of the physical characteristics leads to an objective assessment of the emotion.

- **Match their emotion** with your face, body, breathing and voice tone. You can recall the feeling within yourself by thinking of a time in your life when you felt the same way. There are only four, raw, human emotions, which all of us have experienced with varying degrees of intensity:
  - love/pleasure/joy/sex
  - anger/rage/hate/displeasure
  - fear/guilt/shame/anxiety
  - sadness/misery/grief

- **Express their emotion, with emotion.** A woman is walking frantically out the door saying, "My mother needs me." She is looking up, away from the worker. Her breathing is labored and deep. Her lower lip is pursed. Her shoulders are hunched. Her fingers are clenched. She shuffles towards the door.
  Worker, "You're worried. Is your mother alone?"

- **Ambiguity.** Use "he", "she", "it", "they", "something", or "someone." When people can no longer use dictionary words and you don't understand what they are trying to say, use vague pronouns to substitute for words that you don't understand. You don't need to know the meaning of each word.

> *Resident,* "Flu Flu didn't come home."
> *Worker,* "Do you think something happened to him?"

- **Link the behavior to the need**. Try to find the need that is being expressed and put that into words. The needs most often expressed are:
  - o to be safe/secure/loved
  - o to be useful/working/active
  - o to express raw emotions and to be heard.

A man who was a farmer is looking out the window anxiously and then at the clock. He says, "I have to go home."

> *Worker,* "Do your cows need milking?" She acknowledges his need to be useful.

- **Use music**. Familiar songs learned in childhood and repeated throughout life, become permanently imprinted in their memory. When the V/W sings a well-remembered melody, the time- confused relate immediately.

Example of Validation with Phase Two
Characters: Mrs. Gate, age 96
> Her daughter, age 52, trained in Validation

Place: The daughter's home
Time: 2:00 a.m.

Mrs. G.:	(pulling clothes out of her drawers) It's not here. The noodles are tangled. No room in this tomb.
Daughter:	(touches her mother's arm, looks at her eyes and says in a low, nurturing tone) Noodles? (Rephrase the key word)
Mrs. G.:	My noodles are tangled (points to her head). Get Daddy. Get Daddy.
Daughter:	You mean your brain is tangled? You feel mixed up in your noodle? (Link behavior to the need)

Mrs. G.: Yes. Yes (looks relieved). Daddy can fix my noodle.
Daughter: Daddy always straightened your noodle. You miss Daddy a lot. Were you looking for him just now (points to the drawer)? (Express emotion with emotion, link behavior to the need)
Mrs. G.: He's not here. Nowhere. He left the pants.
Daughter: He left it? (Ambiguity) And you were all alone?
Mrs. G.: All alone.

Daughter: (touching her on the back of her head with her finger tips in a circular motion) When Daddy was with you, you were never alone? You feel alone now. (Touch, express emotion with emotion)
Mrs. G.: (smiles at her daughter)
Daughter: (sings "Take Me Out to the Ball Game", a song her father frequently sang)
Mrs. G.: (sings along, remembering every word)

Mrs. Gate uses vivid images, sharing her feelings of love with her daughter. The genuine caring of the daughter triggers feelings of comfort. One moment of clock-time becomes 50 years of feeling-time.

The daughter continues talking with her mother as she helps her return to bed. She never lies by telling her mother that "Daddy is still alive" nor does she press the facts by saying, "Daddy is dead." Her mother chose to forget that her husband has died. She needs to restore him in order to survive loneliness. Deep down, on the same subliminal level in which a sleeper brushes away a fly, Mrs. Gate knows that her husband is dead.[66] If the daughter had pointed out that painful fact, Mrs. Gate would have withdrawn or become angry. The daughter has replaced Daddy as a symbol of love and security.

The daughter should use Validation for 5 to 10 minutes whenever her mother becomes time-confused. The relationship remains intact; the mother keeps communicating with dictionary words, and does not regress to repetitive motion.

---

[66] Edward Feil, Mrs. Ward, film (Cleveland, Ohio: Edward Feil Productions, 1980)

Techniques for Phase Three: Repetitive Motion

The verbal techniques are only used if, and when the Phase Three person relates on a verbal level.

- **Center** (use as previously described)
- **Use "who, what, where, when, how" questions - never "why."** (use as previously described)
- **Re-phrase.** (use as previously described)
- **Use the preferred sense.** (use as previously described)
- **Polarity,** ask the extreme. (use as previously described)
- **Help the person imagine what would happen if the opposite were true.** (use as previously described)
- **Anchored touch,** where you touch the person is important. Because early, emotionally-tinged memories are permanently imprinted in the brain's circuits, the V/W can kindle a significant relationship by touching Phase Three persons in the same way that they were touched by a loved one in childhood. After 40 years of practice I have found the following:
  - o Using the palm of the hand, in a light circular motion on the upper cheek stimulates feelings of "being mothered", a mother relationship, a familiar "rooting" reflex.
  - o Using the finger tips, in a circular motion, medium pressure, on the back of the head, stimulates feelings of "being fathered", a father relationship, being patted on the head as a small child.
  - o Using the outside of the hand, placing the little finger under the ear lobe, curving along the chin, with both hands, a soft stroking motion downward along the jaw, stimulates feelings of having a "spouse/lover", a sexual relationship.
  - o Using cupped fingers on the back of the neck, with both hands, in a small circular motion, stimulates

feelings of "motherhood or fatherhood," touching a child.

- o Using the full hand on the shoulders and upper back by the shoulder blades, with full pressure, in a rubbing movement, stimulates feelings of "being a sibling or good friend," a brother or sister relationship.
- o Touching with the finger tips on the inside of the calf stimulates feelings of caring for animals, such as horses and cows.

- **Use genuine, direct, prolonged eye contact.** (use as previously described)
- **Use a clear, low, nurturing voice tone.** (use as previously described)
- **Observe the emotion.** (use as previously described)
- **Match their emotion.** (use as previously described)
- **Say their emotion**, with emotion. (use as previously described)
- **Use ambiguity**, the vague pronoun. (use as previously described)
- **Link the behavior to the need.** In this phase the need for love is often expressed by folding, rocking, or pursing the lips to make a clucking sound. The need to feel useful is expressed by moving familiar muscles that were used in working. The need to express raw emotion is expressed by shouting, swearing, pounding, or crying. Please refer to the list of symbols that are on page 78, they are particularly important when people act out rather than verbalize.
- **Use music.** When people don't use speech, the V/W can communicate through singing familiar songs, prayers, familiar, early-learned poems and nursery rhymes.
- **Mirroring.** Copy the body movements, breathing, look in the eye, position of the lower lip, hand and feet movements, and any vocalizations. This must be done without judgment, self-consciousness, or patronizing. This is not a game; people in Phase Three are not children. You are trying to understand the

reason behind their behavior, in order to link the behavior to the need: love, identity, or expression of feelings.

- o Example: a man is sitting in a wheelchair, repeatedly pounding his fist into his other, open hand. The V/W approaches him from the front, stoops down to his eye level or lower, and begins to pound her fist into her other hand using the same rhythm and intensity. She picks up his way of breathing (rapid, shallow, or deep), the look on his face and in his eyes. After 30 seconds, the man stops pounding and looks at her. She also stops pounding. There are five seconds of silent eye contact. The worker says, "You're working hard." The man answers, "Damn right."

The Validation Apron was developed particularly for Phase Three people by Isabelle Vardon and Everett Smith, M.D. It is an apron that has various attachments held on with velcro, that the elderly person can work with throughout the day. Each apron is created with the individuals' needs in mind. For instance, a former waitress would have a pocket filled with napkins for her to fold; a former banker would have a folder filled with play money for him to count; a former secretary would have a pad and pen.[67]

Example of Validation with Phase Three
Characters: Mrs. Mint, age 93
Geriatric nursing assistant, age 22, trained in Validation
Place: The nursing home bathroom. Mrs. Mint is walking back and forth anxiously.
Time: 10:00 p.m.
Mrs. M.:   (tears streaming down her cheeks) Fetzlet. Fetzlet. (She looks under the toilet, the sink, the cabinet.)
V/W: (matching Mrs. M.'s breathing, voice tone, her hand and feet movements) They're gone? You can't find them? (Observe the emotion, match the emotion, use ambiguity, mirroring)

[67] The Validation apron is available from Vardon and Smith at Northwood Care Inc., 2615 Northwood Terrace, Halifax, Nova Scotia, B3K 3S5 Canada

Mrs. M:	All gone. I fudet it and it fitzed. (Her crying increases).
V/W:	(touching Mrs. M. on the back of her neck gently) You miss it so much. (The worker's voice reflects Mrs. M's loneliness and despair.) (Anchored touching, match the emotion, say their emotion, with emotion, ambiguity, link the behavior to the need)
Mrs. M.:	(stops moving and looks at the worker, grieving)
V/W:	(holds the eye contact for ten seconds, matching the grief in Mrs. M.'s eyes, puts her arms around Mrs. M. gently stroking the back of her neck and shoulders, begins to sing) "Jesus loves me... (Genuine eye contact, observe the emotion, match the emotion, mirroring, music)
Mrs. M.:	(sings the entire song with the worker. She weeps, then stops crying, smiles at the worker and strokes her hair.) What a nice girl.

Mrs. Mint never cried when her third child died of pneumonia. Her daughter reports that her mother rarely expressed her emotions. In her old age, Mrs. Mint is healing herself by crying for her lost child. Now in Phase Three of disorientation she needs someone to listen as she releases her grief for the first time.

It's hard to let someone stand there and cry, and have the crying get worse. The worker is not hurting the old person by letting them cry. What hurts is allowing the feelings to remain strangled inside. The worker is helping Mrs. Mint make peace. Expression and validation of feelings will relieve them. At the end, the worker is becoming a substitute for Mrs. Mint's child.

Techniques for Phase Four: Vegetation

- **Center**. (use as previously described)
- **Touch**. (use as previously described)
- You can try getting **eye contact**, but it's very difficult. If you get eye contact, you have succeeded. (use as previously described)

- **Use a genuine, nurturing voice tone**. (use as previously described)
- **Use ambiguity**. (use as previously described)
- **Link the behavior to the need**.(use as previously described)
- **Use music**. (use as previously described)

It is very important to know the social history of a person in the Vegetation phase because you have nothing else to go on. The person gives no emotional "affect". There are no outside clues to what is going on inside them. We trust, however, that there is something going on inside them. The Validation goals for Phase Four are to get:

- Eye contact
- Facial movement
- Some type of emotional response: singing, smiling, crying
- Some kind of physical movement: hands, feet

Example of Validation with Phase Four
Characters: Mr. Simons, age 88
          The physical therapist, age 32
Place: In Mr. S.'s room, he is in bed and has a feeding tube.
Time: 10:30 a.m.

Mr. Simons is lying in bed, eyes closed; his breathing is slow and labored. He makes no body movements. His eyes flicker every once and awhile. The worker gently rubs his calf muscles knowing that he was a rancher. She sings "Home, Home on the Range." Mr. Simons' eyelids flicker, but he does not open his eyes. His lower lip curves upward slightly. The worker sings for one more minute and then leaves. She returns three hours later and repeats the rubbing and singing. Mr. Simons opens his eyes. The worker bends down for eye contact and moves close so that Mr. Simons can see her singing. She now touches his cheek gently with the palm of her hand and continues the song. Mr. Simons keeps his eyes open during the song and closes them when she stops. She leaves.

This one-to-one validation should be applied six times a day, for one minute, as long as the person lives. It is best done by a Validation team.

Typical Mistakes and Reactions

This section is to reassure you that even when you feel that you have made a mistake, it can be corrected. Remember, old people are wise; they will forgive your mistakes.

Mistake:	You mistake a Phase One person for Phase Two and begin to talk about emotional issues with a maloriented person.
Reaction:	"Don't you have other things to do?" The person will push you and the topic away, maybe getting angry.
Correction:	Use "who, what, where, when, how." Say, "What do you think **I** should be doing?" This will help change the subject and salvage the relationship.
Mistake:	Touching someone who doesn't want to be touched.
Reaction:	The person flinches and draws back, when you touch him.
Correction:	Know that you are working with a maloriented person who is afraid of intimacy. Use polarity and say, "What bothers you the most about people who butt into your business?" Or, verbalize the behavior, "You are an independent person, aren't you?"
Mistake:	Not touching someone who needs to be touched.
Reaction:	The person doesn't respond to your verbal exploring.

Correction: Touch him or her in the appropriate way for Phase Two or Three. Or if you have been touching them, touch them in a different place; they may not be feeling your touch due to poor circulation.

Mistake: Using a soft, childlike, or harsh voice tone.
Reaction: None, or rejecting.
Correction: Think of someone you love, so that your voice becomes nurturing, adult and reassuring. Check that you're talking loud enough for them to hear you.

Mistake: Positioning yourself outside of the person's range of vision.
Reaction: The person doesn't respond, or continues repetitive pounding, pacing, or crying out.
Correction: Realize that he or she doesn't see you. Move in closer and directly in front of the person. Frequently old-old people have no peripheral vision.

Mistake: Your body movements don't match what you are saying. When a person is trying to leave the building you ask, "Do you have to see your mother?" while at the same time you are curling your fingers around their arm in a restraining way.
Reaction: The person continues to try to leave or shakes you off.
Correction: Acknowledge your own need to restrain them so that they will stay. Put your own needs away and tune into those of the old-old person. Mirror the person's way of walking, pick up their breathing rhythms, the look in their eyes and say the emotion that you see out loud.

Mistake: You see a person who is acting out their anger of grief and ask them, "You seem angry (sad). Let's talk about it."

Reaction: The person ignores you.

Correction: Stop being a therapist, the person doesn't want to be analyzed. Mirror and match his emotion. Use your feelings more. If he can't talk, verbalize his emotions through a song that matches his feelings.

Mistake: Using words that don't match the preferred sense. An old woman says, "That man is making noises all night long." You answer, "What does he look like?"

Reaction: "I don't know, I didn't see him." It is harder for the person to respond to your questions.

Correction: Say, "How loud were the noises? What did it sound like? Was it a banging?"

Mistake: Patronizing the person or lying. A woman says, "I have to see my mother, she's very sick." You answer, "The doctor is there, they're giving her medicine and she'll be fine."

Reaction: "No, No, No. I have to see her right now. She needs me."

Correction: Mirror the emotion and rephrase what she has said using the preferred sense. "You're worried about your mother. Is she very pale?"

Mistake: Well intentioned lying. An old woman says, "I see a man under my bed." You answer, "Isn't he good looking."

Reaction: Withdrawal. Deep down on a subliminal level, the woman knows that there isn't any man under the bed and that you are patronizing.

Correction: Say, "What does he look like?" and move on to other verbal Validation techniques.

Mistake: Trying to analyze or give insight. The resident says, "The one in the kitchen is poisoning my food." You answer, "Does she remind you of your mother?" trying to make the person realize that she is projecting feelings about her mother onto the cook. You have obtained this information from her daughter.

Reaction: "My mother was a wonderful cook! I wish you could have tasted her food."

Correction: Use a different verbal technique. Example: "What does the food taste like? Which meal is the worst, breakfast or lunch?"

Mistake: You don't come back when you say you will.

Reaction: The resident says to another worker, "You can't trust her, she told me she'd be here at 3:30 and now it's 3:50 and she's not here."

Correction: When you return say: "It's a terrible thing to be late. I'm sorry **I** was late. What did you think happened when **I** didn't come? Did that ever happen before?"

Mistake: You are afraid you're going to uncover something horrible that has been hidden, so you don't explore or touch. The person is crying, and you say, "It's OK. Everything is going to be all right."

Reaction: The person either continues crying and doesn't respond to you at all, or they stop expressing their feelings to please you.

Correction: Say, "You were/are crying. Is it very bad?" Trust that very old people will protect themselves and not let you bring up something that they don't want to face.

Mistake: You have worked for a long time with a maloriented person who said there was a drip from the ceiling that wet her bed. The behavior stopped and you stopped visiting her. A year later, after her daughter moved 3,000 miles away the woman again complains about the drip from the ceiling. The mistake is that you stopped visiting her. Even though she didn't need Validation, she needed your relationship. When her daughter left, it triggered an earlier memory of when she lost her controls i.e. became incontinent. The present day fear of losing her child, is the same as the fear of losing control of her bladder. The facts are different, the fears are the same.

Correction: Come back and begin Validation again, this time don't cut off contact when or if, the drip goes away.

PART FOUR: VALIDATION GROUPS

Seven Steps

The basic principle of group work is to provide a safe environment where people learn to trust each other, so that they can:

- express their feelings
- interact with each other verbally and non-verbally
- solve common problems
- perform social roles
- learn controls
- achieve a sense of worth

This principal holds true for all small groups, as well as for Validation groups[68]

A Validation group worker:

- provides a physically safe place to meet, with privacy
- provides a psychologically safe place, where people will not hurt one another
- facilitates interaction between group members
- states simply, using one-syllable words, and sentences without clauses, two alternatives to a problem
- establishes a ritual, a structured beginning, middle and end
- gives familiar social roles to each group member, that restore dignity and do not raise anxiety
- evaluates progress
- coordinates staff support and the necessary materials for each group meeting (program media)

The goals of a Validation group are to stimulate:

- energy
- social roles
- identity

---

68 Margaret E. Hartford, Groups and Social Work, Columbia University Press, New York and London, 1971

- interaction
- verbal behaviors
- social controls
- well-being and happiness

A group should also:
- reduce anxiety
- prevent vegetation
- reduce the need for tranquilizers and restraints
- reduce bum out in the staff and in families

A group works well with people who are time-confused and those who are in repetitive motion. People in Phase Two and Three have little energy or attention span for one-on-one conversations. In a group, people look at each other, sit close, touch each other through dancing and hand-holding. Energy spreads. Groups trigger memories of family roles, of former social group roles and of social controls. People begin to listen and their speech improves. They begin to care about others in the group, modeling the nurturing worker. By sharing common problems, they solve each other's conflicts. They regain dignity through increased control over their lives. They validate each other.

Maloriented persons who are afraid of feelings and cannot face their recent memory loss, do not belong in a Validation group. The worker would have to limit the maloriented, who often whine, complain, or blame other group members for their own failures. Only after a successful one-to-one relationship, can a maloriented person join a group. Maloriented persons can benefit from a reality-based group that does not stress immediate recall of the present day or date; a group that reviews current events; a Resident's Council that recommends changes in management of the facility; a task-oriented group, such as baking, cooking, or flower-arranging; or a Reminiscing group that does not dwell on emotions. (See pages 135-137 for a description of Reminiscing and Reality Orientation groups.)

A maloriented person can become the worker's assistant in the Validation group, but is not usually a group member.

Step 1: Gather information

Assess the phase of resolution just as you would when working with individuals. Observe the physical and psychological characteristics of the potential group members. Use questions that explore the past. Know the people well. Use the Selecting Members for Validation Groups questionnaire and the History and Baseline Behavior form on page 148. The success of your group will depend heavily on how well you know each person.

Step 2: Select Members

In order to select members, you need to know the following about each person:

- What social role would he be comfortable with? A former preacher could be the prayer leader, a former housewife could be the hostess, and a former church choir singer could be the song leader.
- What is your goal for this individual? Be specific, for example: less crying, improved gait, makes eye contact with others, more speech, etc.
- What phase is the person in most of the time?
- What topic or unresolved issue will engage this person: Unexpressed grief over the death of a child? An unhappy Marriage? Loss of a spouse?
- What music does she respond to? Was she active in a church choir, a barber shop quartet, etc?
- What is his capacity for movement? Can he bear weight? You need to know the medical history.
- What is her potential for relationships with other members? Where should she sit? A woman who misses her husband should sit next to a man who misses his wife; an early onset Alzheimer's person should sit next to a nurturing parent type. Use the questionnaire on page 157 & 158, Selecting Members

for Validation Groups. Select five to ten people in Phases Two and Three. You should have the following:

- One Phase Two person with leadership ability (head of a volunteer group, a "club" person, a business person).
- A person with wise, motherly qualities in Phase Two.
- Four to five Phase Two people who like to talk. You can include early onset Alzheimer's patients whose behavior can be predicted and who will not strike others.
- No more than two Phase Three persons. Choose people in Phase Three who respond immediately to the worker's touch. Constant, repetitive motion can destroy the meeting, creating anxiety for the entire group.
- Maloriented people who can assist the worker, for example, as a violin player and is not threatened by disoriented behavior.

Do not include:

- Phase Three people who will not sit down, or cannot stop loud, constant, repetitive motions in the group.
- Severe early onset Alzheimer's patients, in the last stages, whose behaviors you cannot predict. See the section on Alzheimer's Disease, pages 45 & 46.
- Maloriented people or oriented people. They will be afraid or angry and disruptive to the meeting.
- Aphasic elderly who are oriented to present day reality.
- Mentally ill elderly, whose behavior you cannot predict.
- Retarded elderly who are oriented to present day reality.
- Chronically ill old people whose illness is not related to the aging process.

Step 3: Find Roles for Each Member

Roles give structure to the meetings and help each individual to participate. The Welcomer opens and closes the meeting, the Hostess serves the refreshments, the Song Leader leads the group in singing, etc. Roles ought to make the group members feel useful and necessary to the group; roles ought to stimulate old patterns of behavior and feelings of self-worth.

The worker assigns roles that match the background of each individual. Do not continue roles that cause anxiety. A former secretary may not want to take minutes of the group meetings, fearful of failure. She can become the Song Leader, if she enjoys singing. Wrongly assigned roles can be corrected and changed as people change. Roles in a Validation group are best assigned when people spontaneously choose to perform them. A person who hums all the time can become the Song Leader. An angry man who tells everyone to "shut up" can become the Opening and Closing Chairman, who limits other members. A Kleenex-twister can become the Napkin Passer, etc. The worker watches carefully to match the roles to the individuals and must help them assume their roles.

Do not switch roles once the person has performed well. People need the security of performing the same role at each meeting. With security, comes dignity.

Possible Group Roles:

- Welcomer or Chairperson, the task leader who opens and closes each meeting;
- Song Leader, Rhythm Leader, Bandleader;
- Poetry Reader;
- Chair Arranger, Flower Arranger;
- Secretary;
- Emotional Leader, a motherly person who supports Phase Three members when they cry or pound, etc. The emotional leader usually solves whatever problem is being discussed;
- Host or Hostess, to help pass refreshments.

Step 4: Involve the Staff All Departments

You will need the support of your administration and coworkers in order to have a Validation group. You can do individual Validation on your own, but not a group. You need key staff to help with:

- Transporting the group members to and from the meetings.
- Reserving a private place and good time to meet on a regular, weekly basis.
- Providing refreshments and equipment.
- Getting members ready for the meeting, for example: toileting them beforehand, not sedating them before or during the meeting.
- Evaluating the progress of each member.
- Suggesting new members.
- Suggesting topics.
- Maintaining a good atmosphere, for example, not allowing group members to be taken out of the meeting.

Examples of how staff can help:
- The housekeeper warns, "Mrs. G. and Mrs. S. fight. Don't put them in one group."
- The beautician says, "Tuesdays are no good to meet. That's the only day I do their hair."
- The dietician adds, "You can't give them ice-cream. They're diabetic. Try Vita-cream."
- The head nurse, "Why don't you add Mrs. P. She's very motherly."
- The social worker, "We have a new admission that would be perfect, he's in Phase Two of disorientation."
- The nurse's aide, "Mr. Cane doesn't hit me after the group meeting, when I bath him."

Meet each week with the nursing department. Share Validation with family members of the residents, as well as with volunteers who work in the facility. Sometimes family members will object if they see their parent holding a doll, for example. You need to explain the Validation principles and goals to help them understand that their parent is restoring his or her role as a mother or father and not going through a second childhood.

Step 5: Include Music, Talk, Movement, Food

A Validation group includes music, talk, movement and food. It spends different amounts of time on each activity, depending on the group mood and the verbal ability of the group members on that particular day. Although each meeting is different, the same order of events, or ritual, gives a sense of safety to group members and security for the worker, especially in the beginning of forming a group. The ritual gives a group rhythm. Members look forward to meetings. They express themselves through talk, music, and movement. They end the meeting, looking forward to the next one.

Music:

People in Phase Two and Three cannot talk during the entire meeting. Songs stimulate interaction and blood flow, reduce anxiety, increase thinking capacity, give feelings of well-being and happiness. You should begin and end each group meeting with singing. If possible chose songs that relate to the topic. For example, if you are discussing missing a spouse, sing Let Me Call You Sweetheart. The choice of songs should reflect the cultural and religious background of the people in your group. Consider church songs, folk tunes, and romantic songs that correspond to the tradition of group members, not the background of the younger worker. Current popular music will not involve group members. Examples of songs: "Daisy," "You Are My Sunshine," "Let Me Call You Sweetheart," "The More We Get Together," "When Irish Eyes Are Smiling," "I Want A Girl," etc. Group members can accompany the singing with rhythm instruments, such as drums, tambourines, sticks, and finger cymbals. Creating a rhythm band offers additional roles, as well as an opportunity for group members to interact with other residents and staff by playing for them. Songs end the meeting on an up-beat. Always end the meeting with positive feelings.

Talk:

Always have a discussion topic. Phase Two and Three respond best to topics that bring out feelings of love, belonging, fear of separation, anger, struggle for meaning, and identity–the universal feelings.

Suggested topics:

- missing the parent
- missing one's home
- missing one's job
- missing a spouse, sex, intimate love
- fear of being alone
- fear of losing everything
- boredom, loss of identity
- uselessness, need to belong
- struggle to find a reason for life
- anger at uselessness
- anger at rejection, by parents, children, authorities
- love for each other
- childhood pranks
- punishments
- problems with siblings
- friendship
- how to be happy
- what makes someone angry, sad, happy
- getting along with "crazy" people
- what makes someone "crazy"
- what happens in old-old age
- preparing for death
- how to help each other.

Movement:

- Toss a large, soft ball, calling members' names as they catch the ball. Do not expect members to remember each other's name. Toss the ball while singing.
- Each person holds the same elastic ribbon, moving the ribbon to the beat of the music. The worker encourages group members to follow each other's movements. "Mrs. S. is moving the ribbon over her ear. What does that remind you

of, Mrs. S.?" "I'm hanging out my wash." "Let's all move like Mrs. S."

- Try partner dancing, swaying, wheelchair dancing, simple square-dances and circle dances such as "The Hokey Pokey." These create joy, heighten energy and increase feelings of wellbeing, and closeness. People who are in wheelchairs can often stand and sway to music.
- Move scarves to music.
- Toss bean bags.
- Do arts and crafts projects, such as drawing with big crayons, kneading dough or baking. These activities can help the old-old people express their feelings and trigger feelings of self-worth.

Food:

Refreshments provide nurturing, and trigger adult behavior and social roles. In a social atmosphere, people in Phase Three will become motivated to feed themselves, and often this behavior will continue outside of the group. Since the members themselves pass the food, carefully select food that will not spill, choose cookies that are easily eaten, plates that are light, cups that are easy to handle, and fill the glasses half full, so that the hostess will not be embarrassed by spills. What is served depends on the local culture. Juice and cookies are the norm in the United States.

Step 6: Prepare for the Meeting

Before each meeting prepare the following:

- Plan the agenda. Select the songs and music, the topic for discussion, poems, dances, and refreshments.
- Prepare all the necessary materials and the meeting room. Arrange the chairs in a small, close circle. Members cannot see or hear each other in a large circle. Closeness creates energy. Prepare a seating chart for the nursing staff to make sure that people sit next to those that they enjoy being near. Make sure that the worker sits next to the deaf person and the person who needs constant touching and support. Sit opposite the

verbal person and the group Chairman, so that people on the sides will enter the energy flow.

- Do not use a table. Energy cannot spread around a table. They prevent hearing, seeing, and touching each other. Tables isolate. Use a table only for painting, drawing, or arts and crafts.

Seating Arrangement in a Group:
Natural Leader (Chairman/Welcomer)

Dance Leader Phase Two	Hostess Phase Two
Discussion Leader Phase Two	Song Leader Phase Two
Co-worker	Emotional Leader Phase Two
Pacer Phase Three	Deaf person Phase Three

Validation worker

- See each group member before the meeting to remind them of the meeting. Pick up clues for topics at that time. For example: a person may be angry because her roommate sat in her chair. This anger can be expressed and resolved during the meeting.
- See the nursing staff to see if anything unusual has happened that might influence the course of the meeting.
- When planning the topic relate it to a specific group member. Make the topic a specific problem that the group can solve such as: "Mrs. Jones is crying because she misses her mother. How can we help her, Mrs. Smith?" Ask a specific person who you know is verbal and nurturing. Group members will rally round a person with a problem. The worker states the problem clearly

and simply and asks group members to help solve that problem. Conflicts are vital for group interaction. Example:

o Worker: I saw Mrs. Fast this morning. She still looks angry because Mrs. Smith sat in her chair. Let's figure out a way to help Mrs. Fast feel better. Mrs. Fast, tell us what happened?

The worker helps the two women understand each other. The group members give advice. Solving problems leads to feelings of control and self-worth.

* A tense worker cannot tune into disoriented old-old people. In order to be focused, the worker must be relaxed. Relax before and during the meeting. In order to relax:
  o Concentrate on your center of gravity, a spot one inch below the waist.
  o Breathe slowly in through the nose and out through the mouth. Wash the body with your breath.
  o Stop "inner dialogue." Pay attention to your breath. Focus on your "center".
  o Breathe and focus on the "center" for a count of eight.

Step 7: The Meeting

Groups must meet at least once a week, at the same time, in the same place. Meetings can last from 20 minutes to one hour, depending upon the group's energy. Each meeting is born anew. The group has four parts, a birth, a life, a closing, and a preparation for the next meeting.

Birth: Creating energy

* Greet each person in the circle. Use last names to tap adult behavior and show respect. (about 5-7 minutes)
* Mention each individual's role as you move around the circle to remind group members of their social roles.
* Use a caring, energetic, clear, low, resonant voice tone so that everyone can hear the others' names.
* Touch each person. Pick up their body-language cues.

- Bend down for eye-to-eye contact.
- Move close to each person. Severely disoriented people need closeness.
- Listen to each person as you travel around the circle. If one wants to "hang on," assure that person that you will come back to him after you greet the others.
- Seating is very important. Make sure that everyone is in their usual chair.
- Ask the leader to rise (giving them status), and welcome the group. You should sit or kneel to help the leader rise.
- Ask the Song Leader to start the opening song. Sing more songs, read poems, or say prayers. Build energy and closeness.

Life: The verbal part of the group, problem solving

- Introduce the discussion topic or conflict. (about 5-7 minutes) Always help group members make choices by offering alternatives. For example, "Should we talk about mothers or fathers?" Do not ask, "What shall we talk about?" Severely disoriented people will not be able to answer an open question.
- Do not tell group members what to do, but instead present problems for the group to solve. Trust that the group is wise! Ask the Emotional Leader to solve the problem. The Emotional Leader supports other members, offers reasons for their behavior, welcomes the group, bids them goodbye, expresses feelings for the group, and shows concern. The Emotional Leader should be a wise, nurturing old-old person, with a capacity to share wisdom.
- After the problem has been solved by the group, summarize the interactions. "Mrs. Jones you were so helpful when Mrs. Smith cried. You put your arm around her just when she needed it." "Mr. Jones, without your singing we never would have gotten our group started."
- Use movement or do an activity that builds energy in a nonverbal way. Get people up, if they can stand. A co-worker can dance with the people in wheelchairs. Movement often

stimulates verbal ability. You can also do arts and crafts at this time such as: finger painting, mixing dough, planting, working with clay. (about 5-10 minutes)

- The Hostess or Host can now serve refreshments, coffee and cookies for example. (10 minutes) People in Phase Two and three relate freely in a party mood. Social behaviors are stimulated.

Closing: Create an upbeat, intimate "we" feeling. Meetings should always end on an upswing, even if the group has discussed angry or sad feelings.

- Do your closing ritual. (about 5 minutes) The Song Leader leads the closing song. The Welcomer or Chairman closes the meeting.
- Say goodbye to each member and that you are looking forward to seeing them at the next meeting.
- The nursing staff can now help with transporting the members back to their floors. It is important to move members into social situations where there is an on-going activity, such as a day room or dining room. If members are isolated after the meeting, they will feel a greater sense of loss and often will start to yell or exhibit other negative behavior. They feel abandoned after having been a part of a warm, social group.

Preparation for the next meeting:
- After each meeting, fill out the Validation Group Summary Form on page 159, and the Evaluation of Progress Form on page 161. It is important to track the progress of your group for yourself as well as the rest of the staff. Share this information in staff meetings and with patients' family members.
- In between meetings, continue with individual Validation and informal Validation groups on the floor. Nursing staff on all shifts appreciate specific prescriptions for residents. For example:

Name:	Sadie Ford
Prescription:	Fold napkins 3x per day with a nurse's aide

Names:	Mrs. Feld, Mrs. Thomas, Mrs. Field
Prescription:	Sing Daisy, Daisy, and/or You Are My Sunshine 2x per day, with a nurse's aide who enjoys singing, sitting in a close circle.

How to handle difficult members in the group:

When a member yells, pounds, cries, or exhibits other disruptive behavior, stop the ritual and ask the group to solve the problem.

Worker:	Mr. X. is pounding so hard we can't hear each other (looking at the Emotional Leader)
Mrs. S.:	Do you think he's angry at his children?
Leader:	Yes. That's what it is. They hurt his feelings.
Worker:	Would you ask him?

(Mr. X. stops pounding as Mrs. S. approaches him. The group continues to help him free his anger. They end the meeting by singing "The More We Get Together.")

The group gains cohesion and togetherness by solving a problem. If Mr. X. cannot stop pounding, the group can decide to ask the nurse's aide to help him to his room. The group must continue its life. Each meeting presents a problem that the group can solve.

Example of a Validation Group

The worker greets each person in the circle.

Leader:	Welcome to the Tuesday group. Now shape up! No monkey business today.
Song Leader:	"Daisy, Daisy...I'm all crazy."
Mr. T.:	That's right, lady. You are crazy.
Mrs. G.:	I have to go home. Where are my rubbers. Where is my purse. Help!!!

Mr. T.:	You're crazy too, lady. You're all crazy!
Worker:	(stroking Mrs. G.'s arm) I guess we can't sing together because Mr. T feels everyone is crazy. What makes a person crazy?
Mrs. G.:	Having nothing to do. Get me my rubbers. I have to go to work. The company will pay the fare.
Worker:	You miss the company, don't you, Mrs. G. Was it a big company?
Mrs. G.:	Middle size. A Fendall company. Like the symofile curtains. (She points to the curtains.)
Worker:	How do you mean, symo-file?
Mrs. G.:	I file everything in the company. (She pats her purse and stuffs napkins in each compartment.)
Worker:	(patting the purse with Mrs. G.) You are acting like a very efficient file clerk.
Mr. T.:	She's crazy. That's what she is.
Worker:	(filing with Mrs. G.) Mr. T., Mrs. G. was a file clerk. Is it crazy to want to do the job you did all your life?
Mrs. G.:	I am a filer, like Feil here. (The worker's name is Feil and is pronounced like file.)
Worker:	You mean the files in your company are similar to filing here in this company? In my Feil company?
Mrs. G.:	That's right. Simo-file. Feil. File. File.
Worker:	And my name is Feil. File. Feil. You combined the words.
Mrs. G.:	(smiles and nods)
Worker:	That sounds nice, symo-file, and Fendall. What is Fendall?
Mrs. G.:	Memorable friends from the past. The company.
Mr. T.:	I'll heck her with my pecker. Pecker. Pecker. Pecker. Wanna see the heck-pecker, lady? (He unzips his pants.)
Worker:	Mr. T., you are unzipping your pants. Do you miss your wife?
Mr. T.:	You bet your ass. (He stops unzipping his pants.)

Worker:	(to the Emotional Leader) Mrs. H., what do you do when you miss your husband?
Mrs. H.:	I put his picture in the breadbox, so I could talk to him every morning.
Miss J.:	Harry, Harry, Harry, Harry. I miss Harry.
Worker:	Was Harry your lover, Miss J.?
Mr. T.:	Harry's honest as the day is long. His pecker is long. In Detroit Michigan. Honest as his pecker. My wife is a bitch. A bitch, lady.
Worker:	Did your wife make you angry? What did she do?
Mr. T.:	She is a wooden doll. A doll of wood. She makes coffins. I died last year a thousand deaths.
Worker:	She's a doll of wood and she made you die and still you miss her. Miss J., you miss Harry, whom you loved. Mrs. G., you miss the company which you love, and the companions in the company. What can we do to help each other feel better here in this group, with each other?
Miss J.:	We can help each other.
Worker:	Can we get closer by holding hands and singing and moving together?

The group moves to the ending ritual. The worker has helped the group solve the problem of missing a loved one. The worker emphasizes the good feeling of being together. Note that sexual feelings are dealt with openly. Everyone's sense of loss is expressed tying the group together with a common feeling.

Termination: When a Worker Leaves the Group or a Group Member Dies

People in Phase Two and Three do not always mourn death. They often have come to terms with dying. When a group member dies, acknowledge the death and find a replacement using the recommendations of other staff members. Usually group members will not remember the person who is gone.

Phase Two and Three can end a relationship without being hurt. The worker is easily replaced, providing a new worker listens, touches and validates. It is those qualities that are remembered from week to week and not so much a matter of personalities. Disoriented old-old substitute people. A new worker will be quickly accepted. The departing worker should introduce the replacement at a farewell party to ease the transition. When I left my group that had been going for 10 years, the group members simply said: "Bye!" They easily transferred their trust to the person who took my place. Whenever you leave, always be honest. Tell the people when you are coming back, if you are coming back. Admit your own loss when you leave.

Working with a Co-leader or Co-worker

Since I first began running Validation groups in the '60's, I've learned that working with at least one other person makes for more consistency, reduces the group leader's stress level and offers greater opportunity for feedback and growth. When I began there was no one who helped me bring group members to the meeting, nor helped bring them back to the dining room afterwards. I had no one to reflect with after the group. When I was ill or had vacation, the group simply didn't meet and when I began again, momentum had been lost.

A co-leader has very specific tasks which can include all or some of the following:

- Assist in bringing people to and from the meeting.
- Help with the movement/activity section of the program.
- Sit next to the person who needs extra assistance i.e. is in repetitive motion and needs frequent touch, someone who is deaf and needs many things repeated, someone who is blind and needs extra information whispered, etc.
- Take people out of the group if they become disruptive.
- Help evaluate progress after the meeting and give feedback to the group leader.

- Help choose a topic and plan the next meeting.
- Take over the leadership of the group when needed or planned.

A co-leader should be very present at each meeting - concentrated, carefully observing everyone in the group and be energized. Because the co-leader is usually placed next to someone who has low energy, it is her job to keep an energy flow going around the circle. Some co-leaders talk a lot and some very little, depending on the personal style of the group leader. The two should be in balance. It should always be clear to the group members that the group leader is actually leading the group. If the co-leader takes too much attention, it can become confusing for the group members. One leads, the other supports.

I've had very good experiences alternating who leads the group from week to week. One week I lead the group, the next week the co-leader becomes the leader and I have a chance to be the co-leader. This does not seem to confuse the group members at all. They accept the different leaders when both are empathetic, validating, honest and caring. The same holds true for working with teams. In one institution I know of, Validation groups are run by a team of six people. Each week three of the six are present. One person leads the group and the two others assist. This works very well when everyone in the team has been trained in Validation. The advantages for working in a team are many. If one person is ill, the others can fill in which makes for greater consistency for the group members. When one person has vacation, the group can still meet regularly. People who work in rotating shifts can still take part in the group work when they are scheduled to work on 'group days'. There is more flexibility for management when planning schedules.

A key element of being a co-worker/leader is giving feedback to the group leader. A group leader cannot see everything that goes on during a group meeting and the 'co' offers an important extra pair of eyes both during the meeting and afterwards. During a meeting a co-worker can call attention to a group member who needs some attention when the group leader is otherwise focused. After the meeting the 'co' can give feedback to the group leader about what he or she saw, heard or felt. As a group leader it is very comforting to know that there is someone else to help you out.

PART FIVE: OTHER METHODS

Validation is one method among many that are used with disoriented very old people. It is important for Validation Workers to become familiar with other methods because like most things in life, one method cannot be used for each situation or every client. In this chapter I will describe the basic concepts and ways of practicing reminiscence, reality orientation, behavior modification, re-motivation, and sensory stimulation.[69] Diversion, redirection and psychotherapy will be discussed in so far as they are often confused with Validation.

Reminiscence is a method which explores the past history of a client by remembering. The process of remembering can have a therapeutic value and certainly fits into Erikson's 8th stage, integrity versus despair, where the life task includes reviewing one's life in order to find integrity. There are many ways of practicing reminiscence at different levels of intensity. On an individual basis one can talk about the past in a general or personal way, either formally in sessions or more informally during normal interchange. One can create or review photo albums of the client or find other ways of encouraging elderly to talk about the past. Life review is a form of reminiscence therapy that when done by a trained therapist can help clients gain insight into their behaviors and develop new coping methods. On a group level, there are many ways of practice. Drama groups reenact specific scenes from participant's lives; inter-generational groups exchange stories; a reminiscing group which focuses on sharing memories. Faith Gibson in her book *Reminiscence and Recall* (Age Concern, England 1994) lists 10 good reasons for using reminiscence:

- It connects the past with the present.
- It encourages sociability.
- It reduces distance between carers and cared for.
- It preserves cultural heritage.

[69] Information for this chapter was gathered from a number of sources including: Paul K. H. Kim, Serving The Elderly, Aldine de Gruyter, New York, 1991; Irene Burnside & Mary G. Schmidt, Working with Older Adults, Jones and Bartlett Publishers, London, 1994 (3rd ed.); Mildred 0. Hogstel, Geropsychiatric Nursing, Mosby, St. Louis, 1995 (2nd ed.)

- It reverses the gift relationship.
- It enhances a sense of identity and self-worth.
- It helps a process of positive life-review.
- It alters people's perceptions of each other.
- It helps with assessment.
- It can be an enjoyable activity.

Reminiscing requires a certain amount of attention span and enough verbal ability to express the memories, and an awareness of the difference between present and past time. Reminiscing is sometimes effective with maloriented elderly, who trust the worker, but not as effective with time-confused or those in repetitive motion. Reminiscence therapy is different from reminiscing. One of the goals of reminiscence therapy is to provide insight into past patterns of behavior in order to change present patterns of behavior. This is something that Phase Two and Three people are not capable of, nor are they helped by structured analysis. Maloriented people could go into a Reminiscing group, but not into Reminiscence therapy because they do not want to have insight.

Reality Orientation is based on the beliefs that confusion can be prevented and that people feel better when they are oriented to present time and place. Although originally developed for a totally different patient group, over the last 30 years it has been used with disoriented elderly and has become one of the most popular methods used. In my opinion this is because it is easy for staff. Reality orientation (RO) can be used with individuals, with groups or by the entire staff of an institution as a '24-hour' approach. Individual RO is the gentle reminding of the correct answers to questions such as what day it is, what time it is and where the person lives. One can also use 'cues' such as calendars, clocks and signs that clearly state the 'reality'. For example a sign that reads, "You are in Sunny Vale Home for the Aged," or having a picture of each resident by the door of his or her room. An RO group or class meets generally once a day for 30 minutes and relies on the use of clocks and calendars. Participants are encouraged to read and write. The topics are factual and not emotional. The 24-hour approach is the integration of RO principles and practice throughout an institution and includes environmental or architectural factors as well. An example of this would be the use of mirrors in elevators or halls.

While a maloriented person can sometimes benefit from RO, if it is not patronizing, a time-confused person, or a person in repetitive motion will withdraw, become hostile, and begin to wander or show other rejecting behavior.

Behavior modification stems from the belief that all behavior is learned in three ways: respondent conditioning, that is, when one stimulus becomes associated with another (Pavlov's classical learning theory); operant conditioning, that is, negative and positive reinforcement (Skinner's theory); and imitation, that is, watching and copying other's behavior. This theory is applied to disoriented very old people most often in the form of negative and positive reinforcement. Some examples of behavior modification are: ignoring 'negative' behavior such as crying or calling out for help; withholding desert (or some other positive element like participation in the singing group) if a resident continues unwished for behaviors. On the positive reinforcement side, one can sometimes see personnel giving praise or additional attention to residents who display wished for behavior. Often this method is used in an unconscious way by nursing home personnel, although it is sometimes planned and applied in a conscious way.

I have found that behavior modification does not work with disoriented old-old. They are not aware that they are being punished through negative reinforcement and will not remember the positive reinforcement. There will be no long term change because the basic, underlying reason for the behavior is not addressed.

Sensory Stimulation is an umbrella term for many different methods that share a common goal - to stimulate a person on a sensory level, acoustic, visual kinesthetic, gustatory, and smell. Stimulation of the senses helps reduce feelings of isolation, stress and disconnection with the environment. It can range from being a pleasant experience to a trigger for past experiences. Two of the most commonly used methods that fall into this category are: aroma therapy and snoezelen. Both of these methods are used individually rather than in groups. In short, aroma therapy uses various types of scents to stimulate responses. Snoezelen is a method developed in the Netherlands that has been used with psycho-geriatric patients in the last 10 years. The worker tries to enter the world of the client by exposing the client to various (specifically chosen for the particular client) sensory experiences such as colored lights, use of scented massage lotions, bubble baths, music or taped sounds, textured fabrics and so forth.

Snoezelen, when correctly done with great sensitivity and engagement of the worker, can be quite effective with people in vegetation, sometimes with people in repetitive motion and to a lesser extent with those in time confusion. This method however is often misunderstood or not professionally used and then it doesn't work at all or to the detriment of the client.

Diversion, Redirection and the "Therapeutic Lie"

Diversion and redirection are forms of behavior modification that are used to change so-called 'negative' behaviors such as pounding, pacing, crying, calling out. They are also used often when time confused individuals ask for things that cannot be given, "I want to go home now," or "I have to go to my mother." The worker tries to distract the client by presenting alternative ideas, "While we wait, shall we drink a cup of coffee. Together?"

These two ways of working with disoriented elderly may be easy for the caregiver to use and in some cases are effective in the short-term, but because they do not answer the real need reflected by the client, the behavior will always return.

The 'therapeutic lie' was developed out of a misunderstanding of Validation. The caregiver pretends to accept the unrealistic beliefs of a client. For example:

Client: "I need to go to my mother right now."
Caregiver: "She called and said it was okay for you to stay here a while."

Lying to a client breaks down trust. It also does not take into account one of the important Validation principles, 'there are many levels of consciousness.' The client knows on some unconscious level that her mother has passed away. While the client may initially react to this intervention by calming down, she will generally lose interest in the caregiver and the need to 'go to mother' will repeatedly return because the need behind the behavior has not been fulfilled. The need behind the behavior could be the expression of fear of losing her mother, guilt because her mother died alone or a more existential fear of being abandoned.

Psychotherapy
Validation and psychotherapy share many beliefs such as:
* Early learning affects behavior throughout a lifetime.
* People have to want to change; they cannot be forced to change.
* Permanent change happens after there is insight.
* People feel better when they have expressed their emotions to a trusted listener.

They also share the following goals:
* To increase self-esteem.
* To increase feelings of well-being.
* To help a person cope with stress.

The key difference in these two methods of working is the concept of achieving insight. Maloriented persons do not want to be confronted with their denials and confabulations; they will withdraw or become hostile. A time-confused person or person in repetitive motion does not have the cognitive ability to achieve insight.

ADDENDUM

Implementing Validation on an Institutional Level

Here are some key elements to implementing Validation within a department or institution.

- Accept that not everyone will be interested in or able to do Validation.

- Realize that Validation is one good method, but not the only method that should be used with maloriented and disoriented elderly; not everyone feels comfortable working so intensely with emotions.

- Work with certified Validation teachers or trainers; if the quality of training is not high the results of using Validation might not be positive; get support from an Authorized Validation Organization or center; they have materials, programs and people who can help.

Step 1: Introduce Validation to staff in all departments.

- Give a brief overview of the history, the principles and the goals of Validation. Define the population that does and does not benefit from Validation.

- Show a video or film suggested at the back of this book that clearly demonstrates what Validation is and how it works.

- At the end of the meeting pass around a sign-up sheet for people who want to know more about Validation and want to join your Validation team.

- At a later phase, you will want to have Validation included on a policy level, as part of the interdisciplinary care plan.

Step 2: Form a Validation team.

- If possible include some members from all levels of staff, housekeeping, dietary, administration, maintenance, nursing, social service, recreational therapies, occupational and physical therapy, etc.

- Plan to meet with your team weekly. At first you need to inform them about Validation. They need to learn the phases of resolution and the appropriate Validation techniques for each phase. Use the Individual Validation Session Summary (page 154) and have each team member select an individual with whom they would like to work on an individual basis. Help them to complete the form.

- Each week you need to share your experiences and evaluate your progress. The Evaluation of Progress Form (page 155) will help. During these team meetings you can release feelings about resident that you have not expressed.

- Other staff members will learn by watching you and your team practice Validation and seeing your results.

- After having worked for at least three months with Individual Validation, you can begin planning your Validation group.

Step 3: Begin a Validation group.

If possible, have a co-worker, who can take over whenever necessary. The role of worker and co-worker are interchangeable, but it is important that at each group meeting, there is only one main worker. The co-worker's role is that of support. He or she should:

- help with the movement section of the program;
- assist in bringing people to and from the meeting;
- sit next to the person in repetitive motion;
- take people out of the group if they become disruptive;
- help evaluate progress after the meeting and choose a topic for the next meeting.

The worker and co-worker should support each other on an emotional level as well. Follow the procedures for beginning a group as outlined earlier in Part Four.

Step 4: Begin a Family group.

Three or four times a year, invite family members to an information session about Validation. Keep them informed of their relative's progress in both individual and group Validation. If they are interested, teach the family members specific techniques that will help them communicate more effectively, and improve their relationship with their relative. They will be motivated to visit more often.

Step 5: Review Validation progress with the entire staff every six months.

Authorized Validation Organizations

Validation Training Institute
www.vfvalidation.org
Naomi Feil: naomi@vfvalidation.org
AVO relations and Naomi Feil's Manager:
Vicki de Klerk-Rubin: vdeklerk@vfvalidation.org

There are Authorized Validation Organizations (AVOs) in Austria, Belgium, France, Germany, Italy, Japan, Spain, Sweden, Switzerland, and the United States.
Please visit the following websites for the AVO nearest you:

www.vfvalidation.org
www.validation-eva.com

CHARTS, FORMS, TESTS

Differences in Behavior between Late Onset and Early Onset Demented Populations

EARLY ONSET (45-75 years)	LATE ONSET (80+ YEARS)
Seldom live more than 85 years	Live a long time according to human longevity (90+).
Most have a home, family, social role or position.	Have lost their home, spouse, and social role.
Do not want to withdraw from present reality.	Choose (on a subliminal level) to deny painful losses.
Purposeless, robot-like movements	Return to the past for comfort and to resolve unfinished issues.
Sight, hearing, mobility intact.	Graceful, rhythmical movements.
Eyes remain blank, unfocused when validated or touched.	Deterioration of sight, hearing and mobility.
Ususally will not restore social roles in a Validation group.	Respond with increased orientation to Validation.
Usually cannot control behavior.	Speech often improves and eyes light when validated.
	Adult controls return when validated.
Validation worker cannot establish goals for individual's progress.	
Frustrated in early stages of Alzheimer's when aware of cognitive lossess.	Usually unaware of increasing cognitive losses.
Progressive deterioration until death, regardless of Validation.	Validation worker can establish clear individual goals.
Hit out without provocation.	Deterioration lessens when validated. (Unless individual suffers a stroke or great physical trauma.)
	Often have seizures in the last stages.
Often do not respond to Validation when angry.	
Often cannot swallow.	Deteriorate to vegetation regardless of Validation.
	Will control anger when validated; rarely hit out without provocation.
	Express wisdom.
	Express basic human needs through non-verbal behaviors.
	Often help early onset demented residents, and help each other in a Validation group.

Assessing Observable Behaviors

	Control of Body Functions and Feelings	Eye and Body Movement	Reponse to Losses
Age 80+, oriented, but with physical problem(s).	Wants to feed, dress, and toilet self. Accepts help. Controls feelings appropriately.	Eyes focused, direct, bright. Muscles relaxed, unless paralyzed. Steady, even, sustained gait. Direct movement in wheelchair or walker. Wants to increase range of motion. Aware of loss of control.	Grieves appropriately. Aphasic expresses loss non-verbally. Moves on to new object-relationships, after death of loved ones, loss of job or body-part.
Age 80+, mentally ill.	Can feed, dress, and toilet self. Is unpredictable. Demands or refuses help. Keeps tight control or acts out feelings openly. Can control, if motivated.	Eyes darting or staring. Jaw tight. Face muscles tight. Erratic gait. Stiff movements. Darts in space. Often bent forward when moving.	Cannot expose intimate feelings to a trusted "other." Does not trust. Blames others or self for evil-doing.
Age 45-80, Alzheimer's disease. (Formerly pre-senile dementia seldom lives to 80+).	Overdresses, underdresses; gradually loses ability to dress, toilet, feed. Becomes unaware of angry or sad feelings. Loss is progressive. Cannot understand changes in feelings or intellect. Often has seizures, loses ability to swallow.	Eyes unfocused, blank. Cannot bring finger to tip of nose. Mechanical, robot-like gait. Jerky, awkward movement in space. Purposeless, non-directive walk. Does not move towards an object or person. Uncoordinated.	Aware of loss to thinking centers in early stages. Is not aware of losses in later stages. Denies feelings, possibly due to lack of awareness.

Age 80+, Phase One, Malorientation, occasional confusion.	Can feed dress and toilet self. Wants to hold onto controls and capacities. Confabulates (pretends). Controls feelings rigidly, Seldom expresses feelings.	Eyes focused, direct. Purposeful, rigid, precise movements in space. Precise control of personal belongings. Often stores or hoards to keep control. Fingers pointed, arms folded. Protects self. Keeps self together. Muscles tight.	Denies grief. Denies losses due to aging. Holds onto outworn roles from the past. Denies memory loss. Returns to past conflicts to solve them.
Age 80+, Phase Two, Time Confusion. Phase Three. Repetitive Motion. Phase Two needs help in dressing. Can often toilet and feed self.	Phase Three needs help in all daily living functions. Does not wish to control feelings. Both express feelings freely, to resolve old issues from the past.	Phase Three: bangs, pats, paces, pounds, rocks in even rhythms. Moves loosely in space. Repeats movements. Eyes often closed. Hands clasped or folded. Loses awareness of body in space through sensory damage. Both have loose facial muscles.	Phase Two and Three no longer deny feelings. They express grief, anger, etc. freely. They retreat to the past to survive deep feelings of loss. They panic when aware of losses. They blot out painful reality by re-creating images from the past.

	Response to Rules and Social Norms	Response to Time, Place, Person
Age 80+, oriented, but with physical problem(s).	Accepts social norms. Accepts physical and social limitations. Compromises when wishes cannot be fulfilled. Seeks substitute pleasures. Sublimates sexual and hostile feelings in socially approved channels. Wants approval.	Is aware of clock time. Accepts recent memory loss. Finds ways to keep track of appointments, names, etc. Classifies people and objects appropriately. Compares similar and different objects, using metaphoric speech. Reviews the past. Aphasic re-trains cognitive functions to classify objects.
Age 80+, mentally ill.	Has rejected rules throughout life. Has often been hospitalized. Cannot hold a job. No intimate "gut-level" friends. Delusions, images, and hallucinations based on fabricated people & objects, not on loved ones from the past.	Names and classifies correctly. Knows clock time. Feels others hurt them. Fabricates people and objects. Fears are not related to aging, they have been going on for a lifetime.
Age 45-80, Alzheimer's disease. (Formerly pre-senile dementia. Seldom lives to 80+).	Tries to hold onto rules and social skills in early stages. Conforms in early stages. Wants to dress well. Performs in a ritualistic, mechanical way. In last stage, can no longer perform. Is unaware of rules. Has no insight into loss of social skills.	Loses track of time, place and person. Is aware of losses in early stages. Loses track of names and roles of loved ones. In unaware of losses in later stage. Loses ability to use and name objects. Loses recognition and cognition.

Age 80+, Phase One, Malorientation	Holds onto rules. Keeps track of social obligations. Is threatened by those who do not follow rules. Wants things in place according to specifications. Wants approval of authority. Hoards.	Is aware of present time, place and person. Is frightened by occasional recent memory loss. Wants to think clearly. Uses humor to cover losses. Wants to justify the past; to sum up life.
Age 80+, Phase Two, Time Confusion Phase Three, Repetitive Motion	No longer wants to conform to social rules. Retreats. Blots out present authority's rules. Does not want approval of present caregivers. Wants approval of past loved ones and turns to significant others from the past for rules of behavior. Restores early childhood rules. Will not modify behavior unless motivated.	Does not use clock time. Measures time by memories. "Sees" people and places from the past in vivid images. Replaces damage to sight, hearing and movement with "inner-sight","inner-hearing", and memories of moving in the past. Relives and restores the past to resolve living and regain identity.

	Verbal Communication	Non-Verbal Communication, Use of Symbols	Appropriate Group
Age 80+, oriented with physical problem(s).	Communicates to gain understanding. Uses humor. Verbally ties past with present to gain integrity. Wants to be understood.	Aphasic uses eye contact and gestures to communicate. Low, even relaxed voice-tone. Keeps personal distance, unless intimate with family. Can read and write, although is often shaky.	Task-oriented, such as: baking, art, music, pottery, writing, humor group (Ah ha," brings a belly laugh, "Ha ha," restores well-being.)
Age 80+, mentally ill	Seldom listens. Answers according to mood. Names people and objects correctly. Rambles or is silent. Speaks in harsh, whiny tones.	Avoids direct eye contact. Avoids touch. Acts out instinctive needs. Little metaphoric thinking. Switches people and objects	Remotivation groups with objective stimuli; Reality orientation that is not patronizing. Caring workers help mentally ill people.

Age 45-80 Alzheimer's disease, (Formerly, pre-senile dementia, seldom lives to 80+)	Speech is garbled. Cannot classify objects. Forgets names. Does not connect thoughts. Cannot make choices.	Does not recall touch. Uses hand gestures. Random movements. Cannot read or write.	A Validation group can stimulate interaction. Trips to familiar spots can stimulate dormant speech and wellbeing in early stages.
Age 80+, Phase One, Malorientation	Wants verbal reminder of time and place. Uses dictionary words, complex sentences, humor, sarcasm, repeats same stories. Seeks facts to understand.	Controls eye-contact. Avoids touch. Keeps personal distance. Uses symbols to express old conflicts (see page 76) Reads and writes.	A political discussion group gives an outlet for hostility. A task oriented group, non-patronizing Reality Orientation group and Remotivation group help maintain well-being.
Age 80+, Phase Two, Time Confusion Phase Three, Repetitive Motion	Blends sounds, to form unique, personal words. There is little use of dictionary words. Returns to early emotionally tinged words and sounds, rhymes. Restores the past through forming sounds. Cannot use logical, as-if reasoning. Cannot use metaphors.	Body parts, objects and people in present time, become people and familiar objects from the past. Feelings are freely expressed. Communication is largely non-verbal. Often reads, but cannot write.	Validation groups acknowledge feelings; respect the need of old-old people to restore the past when the present has lost meaning. Well established social roles return. Stress lessens. Gait improves. Dormant speech can return, social interactions produce well-being. They will not vegetate.

The Stage Beyond Integrity: Feil's Resolution versus Vegetation Stage

	Phase One: Malorientation	Phase Two: Time Confusion	Phase Three: Repetitive Motion	Phase Four: Vegetation
Basic Helping Cues for the Care-Giver	- use who, what, where, when and how questions - use minimal touch - maintain social distance	- use preferred sense - use touch and eye contact - use ambiguous pronouns - match their emotions	- use touch, eye contact - mirror emotions and movements	- mirror movement - use sensory stimulation - use music
Orientation	- keep track of time - hold onto present reality - realize and are threatened by own disorientation	- do not keep track of clock time - forget facts, names, places	- shut out most stimuli from outside world - have own sense of time	- do not recognize family, visitors, old friends or staff - no time sense
Body Patterns: *Muscles*	- tense, tight muscles - usually continent - quick, direct movements - purposeful gait	- sit upright but relaxed - slow, smooth movements - dance-like gait	- slumped forward - unaware of incontinence - restless, pacing - repeats early childhood movements and sounds	- placid, slump - little movement, fetal position - no effort to control continence - frequent finger movements
Vocal Tone	- harsh, accusatory, and often whining - can sing	- low, rarely harsh - sing and laugh readily	- melodic - slow and steady tone	
Eyes	- focused, good eye contact	- clear, unfocused - downcast, eye contact, triggers recognition	- eyes usually closed	- eyes shut (face lacks expression)

Emotions	- deny feelings	- substitute memories and feelings from past, to present situations	- demonstrate feelings openly	- difficult to assess
Personal Care	- can do basic care	- misplace personal items - need help with basic care	- cannot care for themselves	- cannot care for themselves
Communication	- communicate clearly - use dictionary words	- begin to use unique word combinations - have difficulty with nouns	- communicate mainly on a nonverbal level - substitute movement for speech	- difficult to assess
Memory and Social Behavior	- some short-term memory loss, which they find disturbing - can read and write - conform to rules and conventions	- have "selective" memory, mainly long-term - can read, but no longer write legibly - create up own rules	- early memories and universal symbols are the most meaningful - cannot read or write - have no rules	- difficult to assess
Humor	- retain some humor	- cannot play games with rules (Bingo, etc.) - unique humor	- laugh easily, often unprompted	- difficult to assess

History and Baseline Behavior

Resident's Name: _____

Personal Information: age, sex, race, birthplace, employment history, children, etc.	Family background, socio-economic and religious background, dose family relationships (names).
Health Information: medical diagnosis, length of hospitalizations, medications, physical losses.	In This Home: Friends? Activities? Movement? Relationship to staff? Night-time behavior vs. day time. Eating behavior.
Action Patterns: Customary response to crisis, losses. What precipitated hospitalization? What is the preferred sense? Typical relationships. Physical behavior: muscles, movement in space, eye contact, response to touch.	Typical emotional patterns. Expresses feelings? Denies feelings? Which feelings are most often expressed? (anger, love, fear, grief)
Phase of resolution: Malorientation? Time-confusion? Repetitive motion? Vegetation? Psychotic behavior? Fluctuates between phases?	Recommended Validation treatment: Individual? Group? Give details. What role? Where should they sit?

153

Individual Validation Session Summary

Validation worker: _____

Client's name: _____

Date: _____

Time/length of session: _____

Phase of Resolution: _____

What happened?
(Songs? Symbols? Which techniques were used?)

What did I find easy?

What did I find difficult?

Individual Validation Evaluation of Progress Form

Fill out this form after each group or individual meeting. Rate each person as follows: NAME OF CLIENT:
0 - never; 1 - rarely; 2 - occasionally; 3 - frequently; 4 - always.   NAME OF VALIDATION WORKER:

Date	Phase of Resolution at the beginning and end of session	Verbal interaction	Makes eye contact	Allows for touch	Typical behavior patterns*	Typical behavior patterns*	Typical behavior patterns*	(other)	(other)

* Each client has his or her personal behavior patterns usually associated with the coping mechanisms used to deal with difficulties in life. Some of these behaviors are difficult for others to handle. Through Validation one can try to reduce these 'difficult' behaviors. To evaluate the effectiveness of Validation, list specific, typical behavior patterns at the top of the column (examples: pacing, hoarding, crying, yelling 'Police') and rate the frequency of the behavior after every Validation session.

Selecting Members for Validation Groups

Questions for staff and family members. "Yes" answers indicate a Phase One level of disorientation. Seven or more "yes" answers indicate a life time of mental illness. Do not include either in a Validation group.

1. Has the person ever been admitted to a mental hospital?
2. Does this person blame others for physical losses?
3. Does this person blame others for social losses?
4. Does this person know where he/she lives?
5. Does the person know where he/she lived before? The names of his/her children? The names of staff members?
6. Does this person have a history of retardation?
7. Does the person remember an intimate relationship with someone he/she loved, but blames this person for his/her losses?
8. Has the person been unable to form an intimate relationship?
9. Does the person hold onto rules rigidly?
10. Is the person wary of expressing feelings?

Seven or more "yes" answers to the following questions indicate aphasia or organic diseases that do NOT accompany normal aging. Do not include this person in a Validation group.

1. The person uses correct speech, omitting small connecting words, such as "and, but, I, they, up, down," etc.
2. Cries when happy, laughs when sad.
3. Swears constantly.
4. Is rigid in body movement, mechanical (without drugs.)
5. Dresses well, is socially correct, but NOT oriented to present time.
6. Understands what is said, but cannot express him or her.
7. Has a sense of humor.
8. Can read a newspaper.
9. Can play bingo, or games with rules.
10. Does not make eye contact or respond to nurturing touch.
11. Does not respond to caring voice tone.

Questions to ask residents. Repeated references to the past indicate Phase Two or Three.

1. Who do you miss most? Your spouse? Your children?
2. What did you do to earn a living?
3. Did you mind leaving your home to move here?
4. What is the worst thing about getting old?
5. How do you overcome sadness?
6. What is the most important thing in life?
7. What happened to you that brought you here?
8. Do you have a lot of pain? (Phase Two and Three often do not complain of pain as often as more oriented residents.)
9. Were you in a hospital? What did the doctors do?
10. Do you like the other people here? If not, why?
11. Do you like the staff? Who don't you like? (Phase Two and Three will say they live at "home" and do not recognize staff.

Validation Group Summary

Date: _____ Name of Group: _____

Validation worker: _____

INVITATION TO GROUP MEETING
TODAY: (list unusual responses)

MAIN ISSUES AND EVENTS:

PLANS FOR NEXT MEETING:

COMMENTS AND RECOMMENDATIONS:

Validation Group Summary   *SAMPLE*

Date: 3/8/91   Name of Group: The Tuesday Group

Validation worker: N. Feil

INVITATION TO GROUP MEETING TODAY:
(list unusual responses)

Mrs. Smith refused to come. She looks very sick
Mr. Stout kissed me.

MAIN ISSUES AND EVENTS:

Discussion of sexual needs, missing husbands and wives. Mr. Stout misses his wife. He will become either the Host or Head Dancer to fill his needs to be with women.

PLANS FOR NEXT MEETING:

Topic: death of a parent.
Songs: "Jesus Loves Me," "I want a Girl," "Rock a Bye Baby"
Problem to solve: When you're lonely and miss your parents, what can you do?

> Ask Mrs. Tubin if she prays or looks for friends.
> Other solutions: sing a lullaby, take a walk, read a poem, remember your mother

Movement: rocking to music holding a big elastic band.
Refreshments: coffee and cookies

COMMENTS AND RECOMMENDATIONS:

Find out from the head nurse if Mrs. Smith has heart trouble. Let Mr. Stout sit next to Mrs. Cone. Encourage them to dance. Get "Let Me Call You Sweetheart" record. Next meeting, celebrate Mrs. Smith's 90th birthday. Topic: getting older

Validation Group - Evaluation of Progress Form

Fill out this form after each group or individual meeting. Rate each person as follows:
0 - never; 1 - rarely; 2 - occasionally; 3 - frequently; 4 - always.

Date	Name	Phase	Talks	Makes eye contact	Touches	Smiles	Takes Leadership role in group	Participates (physically): dances, sings.	Other, personal behavior. Comments and notes for the next meeting.

Evaluating Your Validation Skills

The following tests can be given to evaluate potential Validation workers (people who will be working with Alzheimer's type populations) in an institution or organization.

Circle the correct answer.

1. A disoriented resident screams every time she drops her purse. Should you:
   (a) Try to make sure she has the purse. Explore to build trust. Find out what the purse means to her.
   (b) Assure her that she has no need for the purse in this place. She isn't going anywhere. She doesn't need money.
   (c) Take her purse away. "Out of sight out of mind."

2. A disoriented old-old man unzips his pants in public. Should you:
   (a) Gently walk with him to his room, and ask, "Do you miss your wife?"
   (b) Negatively reinforce him. Firmly let him know, "We don't do things like that around here."
   (c) Mirror his actions.

3. A disoriented resident hollers, "**I** want my teeth!" Should you:
   (a) Find out where her teeth are, or get her false teeth if needed.
   (b) Tell her that she always takes her teeth out and loses them.
   (c) Tell her she is too old for new dentures.

4. When you are with a disoriented person, are you most inclined to:
   (a) Keep your distance.
   (b) Touch them softly to elicit interaction.
   (c) Stand close without touching.
   (d) Use soft touch together with close eye contact.

5. When a person is in Phase Three (repetitive motion), you should:
   (a) Mirror their actions using touch and close eye contact.
   (b) Ask them what they are doing.
   (c) Ask them to stop.
   (d) Ignore their actions.

Please mark either (T) True, or (F) False.

6. ( ) Almost all old-old people who are disoriented are incontinent.

7. ( ) All old people ought to know their married name, where they are, the present date and time.

8. ( ) People who live in the past are happy that way, so it's better to pretend to believe them.

9. ( ) People who are over 80 years old and disoriented, with physical failures and social losses, turn to the past to resolve old conflicts and to restore old pleasures.

10. ( ) It is important to correct disoriented people when they are mistaken or forgetful.

11. ( ) It is important for older people to have alternative interests to prevent withdrawal.

Please answer the following in essay form. Use additional paper.

12. List Erikson's life stages and their related tasks.
13. Identify and describe the four phases of resolution.
14. Describe the goals and needs of old-old people in each of the four phases.
15. Describe the Validation techniques that are useful for each phase of resolution.
16. List the steps involved in centering yourself.
17. List the steps necessary in forming a Validation group (for the first time).
18. Write a brief introduction of Validation, as you might present it to family members or staff.

Answers to questions 1-11 are on page 165.

Validation Homework Assignments

The following forms can be used to help train co-workers or family members in the use of Validation techniques.

Assignment 1 Discover the preferred sense of the following persons and justify your "diagnosis" by stating clues that tipped you off.

a) Your partner (or other intimate person):
Preferred sense:

Clues:

b) Your child:
Preferred sense:

Clues:

c) A co-worker:
Preferred sense:

Clues:

d) A resident:
Preferred sense:

Clues:

e) Resident #2:
Preferred sense:

Clues

Assignment 2: List as many words as you can which can serve as responses when talking with a person identified as having the following preferred sense.

Hearing	Seeing	Feeling

These assignments were created by Mary Bayer, R.N.
Sandy River Alliance Nursing Care Centers in Portland

Answers to the Evaluating Your Validation Skills Quiz

Question	Answer
1	a
2	a
3	a
4	d
5	a
6	T
7	F
8	F
9	T
10	F
11	T

TO THE READER:

This is a sample of handwriting is typical of disoriented Old-Old people moving from stage one to stage two Families and Staff can learn to recognize the change in handwriting as one way of assessing the stage of disorientation.

Bibliography

American Psychiatric Association, *Diagnostics and Statistical Manual of Mental Disorders IV, Washington DC, 1994*

L. Babins, J. Dillion, S. Merovitz, The effects of validation therapy on disoriented elderly, *Activities, Adaptations & Aging* 12 (1989): 73-86

R. Bandler, J. Grinder, *Frogs into Princes: Neuro linguistic Programming;* Real People Press, Utah, 1979.

Robert N. Butler and Alexander G. Bearn (eds.), The Aging Process, Therapeutic Implications, Raven Press, New York, 1985

J. T. Dietsch, L.J. Hewett, S. Jones, Adverse effects of reality orientation, Journal of American Geriatric Society 37: 974-976

Erik H. and Joan Erikson, *The Life Cycle Completed,* extended version, W.W. Norton & Co., New York, 1997

Naomi Feil, Group Therapy in a Home for the Aged, *The Gerontologist* 7 (1967): 192-195

N. Fell, J. Flynn, Meaning behind movements of the disoriented old-old, *Somatics 4 (1983): 4-10*

Naomi Feil, Resolution: The Final Life Task, *Journal of Humanistic Psychology 25 (1985): 91-105*

Naomi Feil, Validation: An Empathetic Approach to the Care of Dementia, *Clinical Gerontologist 8 (1989), No.3*

N. Feil, Validation Therapy, in: P. K. H. Kim (ed.), *Serving the elderly,* Aldine de Gruyter, New York, 1991: 89-115

N. Feil, Validation therapy with late onset dementia populations, in: G. Jones, B.M.L. Miesen (eds.), *Caregiving in dementia,* Routledge, London, 1992: 199218

N. Feil, When Feelings Become Incontinent: Sexual Behavior in the Resolution Phase of Life, *Human Sciences Press (Special Issue Sexuality and Aging)* 13 (1995): 271-282

N. Feil, Current Concepts and Techniques in Validation Therapy, in: M. Duffy (ed.), *Handbook of Counseling and Psychotherapy with Older Adults,* John Wiley and Sons, New York, 1999: 590-613

Naomi Feil, Validation Therapy, in: Mezey et al. (eds.), *The Encyclopedia of Elder Care: The Comprehensive Resource on Geriatric and Social Care,* Springer Publishing Co, New York, 2000

Naomi Feil, *The Validation Breakthrough,* Health Professions Press, Baltimore, 2002 (2nd ed.)

J. Fine, S. Rouse-Bane, Using Validation Techniques to Improve Communication with Cognitively Impaired Older Adults, *Journal of Gerontological Nursing* 21 (1995): 39-45

Sigmund Freud, *The Basic Writings of Sigmund Freud, vol. I: The Psychopathology of Everyday Life*, Random House, New York, 1938: 35-150

Howard Gardner, *The Shattered Mind,* International Universities Press, New York, 1949

Herbert Ginsburg and Sylvia Opper, *Piaget's Theory of Intellectual Development,* Prentice-Hall, Englewood Cliffs, N.J., 1969

R. Gordon, *Your Healing Hands:* The Polarity Experience, Unity Press, Santa Cruz, Cal., 1978

Charles Hampden-Turner, *Maps of the Mind,* Macmillan Co., New York, 1981
R.D. Laing, *The Divided Self* Penguin Books, Baltimore, 1969

C. Lewis, N. Feil, Validation Techniques for Communicating with Confused Old-Old Persons and Improving their Quality of Life, *Geriatric Rehabilitation 11:* 34-42

I. Morton, C. Bleathman, Validation Therapy: extracts from 20 groups with dementia sufferers, *Journal of Advanced Nursing* 17 (1992): 658-666

Frederick Munsch, *Prise en Charge des Troubles Psycho-comportementaux Chez des Personnes Agees en Institution*, Atteintes de Deficiencies Cognitives, Faculte de Medicine, Universite de Limoges, (2000).

idea-l and Tertianum ZfP, 2004, *Evaluationsstudie über die Praxiserfolge von Validation nach Feil am Beispeil eines Tertianum ZfP Validation Anwenderseminars*. Retrieved from **https://vfvalidation.org/validation/Gunther_EvaluationsstudieUberDiePra x.pdf**

Robert E. Ornstein, *The Psychology of Consciousness,* Harcourt Brace Jovanovich, New York, 1977

Karl H. Pribham, *Languages of the Brain,* Wadgworth Publishing Co., Monterey, Cal., 1977

Carl Rogers, *Counseling and Psychotherapy,* Houghton Mifflin Co., Boston, 1942

Carl Rogers, *Way of Being,* Houghton Mifflin Co., Boston, 1981
Charles Wells, *Dementia,* F.A. Davis Co., Philadelphia, 1977

I. Welwood, Befriending Emotion, *The Journal of Transpersonal Psychology* 11 (1979), No. 2: 145

Zepelin, Wolfe and Kleinplatz, Evaluation of a Yearlong Reality Orientation Program, *The Journal of Gerontology* 36 (1981), No. 1: 70-77

Edward Feil Productions Films and Videos

Where Life Still Means Living, Montefiore Home, 1964 (24 min F&V).

The Inner World of Aphasia, Montefiore Home, 1968 (24 min. F&V). *The Tuesday Group, Montefiore Home,* 1972 (14 min. F&V).

When Generations Meet, Montefiore Home, 1973 (24 min. F&V).

A New Life for Rose, C. Schnurmann Housing, 1973 (24 min. F&V).

Living the Second Time Around, 1974 (22 min. F&V).

Looking for Yesterday, Cleveland, 1978 (29 min. F&V).

100 Years To Live, Cleveland, 1981 (29 min. F&V).

My First Hundred Years, Cleveland, 1984 (57 min. V).

The More We Get Together, Cleveland, 1986 (44 min. V).

Act Your Age: Marge the Blamer; Muriel the Wanderer; Cleveland, 1988 (21 min.V).

Communicating with the Alzheimer Type Population: the Validation Method, Cleveland, 1988 (19 min. V).

Sarah's Choice, Cleveland, 1992 (10 min. V).

V=Video, F=Film

Index